GAMBLE TO WIN CRAPS

R. D. Ellison

Lyle Stuart
Kensington Publishing Corp.
www.Kensingtonbooks.com

To Sharon Joan Pfeiffer

Lyle Stuart books are published by

Kensington Publishing Corp.
850 Third Avenue
New York, NY 10022

All Kensington titles, imprints, and distributed lines are available at special quantity discounts for bulk purchases for sales promotions, premiums, fund raising, educational, or institutional use. Special book excerpts or customized printings can also be created to fit specific needs. For details, write or phone the office of the Kensington special sales manager: Kensington Publishing Corp., 850 Third Avenue, New York, NY 10022, attn: Special Sales Department, phone 1-800-221-2647.

Lyle Stuart is a trademark of Kensington Publishing Corp.

First printing February 2001

10 9 8 7

Printed in the United States of America

ISBN 0-8184-0621-6

TABLE OF CONTENTS

TABLE OF CONTENTS

TABLE OF CONTENTS

PART II: PROFESSIONAL TECHNIQUES

TABLE OF CONTENTS

TABLE OF CONTENTS

TABLE OF CONTENTS

INTRODUCTION

All the craps tables in the Frontier casino were filled, except for an opening next to the stickman at the middle table. Without hesitation, I grabbed the spot.

The player to my right immediately caught my attention. A big, noisy biker type with tattoos, metal studs on his outfit and hair halfway down his back. But it was his *chips*—not his appearance —which caught my eye. He had a couple thousand dollars in greens in his tray, and a stack of red chips fifteen inches high, representing his bet, on the don't pass line. Every so often he'd toss a nickel to the stickman, saying, *"Big Red for the shooter,"* trying to encourage a seven-out.

As the dice moved around the table, I watched his technique, with a bizarre mixture of loathing and admiration. At the beginning of each shooter's roll, he covered all of the non-point numbers for $50 each, and collected two to three hundred dollars from those before pulling them down and waiting for the seven-out, which would net him several hundred dollars more.

Shooter after shooter, he continued to play on that basis, as the trend obligingly held up.

When the dice reached his two pals just ahead of him, he switched his bets from the *Don't* side to the *Do* side. *"Bad move,"* I said to myself, knowing that capricious favoritism has no place at the craps tables. Didn't matter. He won all those bets as well. Then the dice came to him.

He bet on himself the same way he did for his buddies, betting the pass line for the first point attempt, and don't pass for the second. The man could not lose. Every bet he made was as golden as the inside of Fort Knox.

When the dice came to me, he upped his *don't* bet to a stack of greens as high as his previous stack of reds. I was trying to hide my glee when I rolled a come-out seven and watched the dealer pull his stack away, but he didn't even blink. He just created another pile of greens, even higher than the last. In the end, I didn't disappoint him.

He was there to win. And he did.

Later on, he got into an argument with the boxman, who had started to complain that his chip piles were too high, for his stacks on the don't pass had grown to where they were unstable. The biker, trying to get his way, argued that his uncle was a casino executive there at the Frontier, which carried the veiled threat that the boxman's job might be at stake.

I simply could not believe what I was seeing. The crudest, swarthiest player in the whole casino, playing the shrewdest game of craps I had ever seen.

But there is an explanation: it's one more shining example of the unexplainable, which you'll find every day in the casinos.

PART I

THE BASICS

1

A POOL OF SHARKS

Welcome to the world of selective wagering, where casino games are used as vehicles for generating income. Here, you will learn how one can maintain a consistent income by exploiting casino conditions that favor the player, and we will take you there using the most direct route.

The objective of this book is to give you what you need to get started, and to succeed on a continuing basis. You will learn about risk probabilities, systems and procedures, the implications of trends, and the art of building a bankroll.

It doesn't take a genius to understand this book, but you'll be in for the fight of your life, because everything the casinos do is calculated to quickly separate you from your money. It is their job, in fact, to treat you like a celebrity while they systematically plunder the contents of your wallet.

Every time you play, you'll be diving into a pool of sharks. Your goal will always be to get what it is you need from them—before they thrash you to pieces!

This book demonstrates the finer points of casino wagering, with an emphasis on discipline, patience and precision technique. If you stick to the program, you may discover that it offers the best approach that is currently available for waging commercial warfare against the casinos.

A PORTFOLIO OF PLAYS

If you are seeking income and not entertainment from table games, your best bet is to look at a casino as a processing plant. You're the quality control guy on an assembly line. But instead of looking for rejects to be discarded, you're looking for plums: betting opportunities that spring up periodically, offering some indication of future potential at a table.

Table game play, for those who consistently succeed at it, is a methodical process of turning over money, using the games as vehicles for doing so. Given time, a precise table condition will present itself, which is your cue to launch a wagering series. If you confine your bets (only) to those times when the table is sending signals, you'll do better in the long run than those who play randomly and without structure.

The strategy offered in this book is to have a portfolio of plays. That is, a group of wagering devices that are utilized only when table patterns indicate that a specific condition is present. Each of these plays is activated by its own separate wagering trigger. When one appears, this tells you that the table is ripe for a specific bet or betting progression. You won't win every one of these battles, but if you dance from one to the next as conditions dictate, there is a reduced chance that you'll become victimized by a table trend that persists in sending false signals about the viability of any individual strategy.

Some of these plays involve betting with the seven; some involve betting against it. This diversified portfolio will help you capitalize on all types of table patterns, offering the best chance for short term gains, and long range success.

HITCHHIKING AND THE LAW OF AVERAGES

I think I was in the eighth grade when I became aware that a certain group of my classmates favored hitchhiking as a means of transportation home from school. These were the malcontents, who smoked, drank beer, and wore black leather jackets. I never understood why they didn't take the schoolbus like everyone else, but it wasn't any of my business.

Until, one day when an errand happened to take me right past one who had his thumb stuck out, and I decided to strike up a conversation. It became my first exposure to the concept of the *Law of Averages.*

His name was Dennis, and maybe it was because he smiled a lot that I found the nerve to approach him. It hadn't occurred to me that doing so helped him get a ride more quickly.

"Hey Dennis, how's it going?"

"Not bad. . .what's up?" He glanced at me, but was focused on the passing traffic.

"Why're you hitchhiking?" I asked, seeking a quick answer. *"Why not take the schoolbus?"*

"I dunno. . .had some stuff to do. . ." Disdainfully, he flicked an ash from his cigarette. A car filled with girls passed by and he gestured in an attempt to get their attention.

"But. . .what if a car never stops?"

"That never happens." He continued to smile, but kept his gaze fixed straight ahead.

I was exasperated. *"How do you **know** that won't happen? How could you possibly know that?"*

He shrugged. *"I always get a ride after 20 minutes or so."* Our discussion was boring him.

I looked at him with disbelief. How could he be so sure a ride would come? Then I thought about the timeframe. Imagine that! No matter where he was or what time it was, the car that would end up giving him a ride was twenty minutes away, making its way toward him like clockwork. It was a game of chance he always won.

At the time, that kind of thinking was incomprehensible. Never would it have occurred to me to put unconditional trust in such an expectation. But Dennis appeared confident enough to convince me that he would succeed.

A few years later I tried it myself and found he was right. Sooner or later, a ride would come. But it probably averaged out to twenty minutes, like he said.

What I learned since then is that in affairs of chance, it's only a matter of time before the *Law of Averages* intercedes and begins to impose its will. Because, in support of that law, there lies a statistical imperative:

Given time, events will seek their proper place within their assigned probabilities.

Because of this, it would not be possible for an even, unbiased result, derived from, say, the flip of a coin, to win 500 consecutive decisions.

Sorry. Not possible.

Now, everyone knows that the cards and dice do not think for themselves. Therefore, every table decision is independent of the one before and the one after. But if this is true, where does the Law of Averages step in? Somewhere along the line, events are compelled to move toward their inherent probabilities. And this means that these events, when viewed in groups, are bending to a preordained will.

Exploitation of this phenomenon is the task of the gambler. Conveying its intricacies is the task of this book.

THE PATIENCE IMPERATIVE

A man was having a dialogue with God: *"Dear God, in your infinite wisdom, what is a million years to you?"*

Replied the voice from above, *"A million years is but one minute to me."*

The man persisted: *"Lord of the universe, in your infinite knowledge, what is a million dollars to you?"*

"A million dollars is but one penny to me."

"Well then, benevolent one," he said, *"in your infinite generosity, could you grant me one of your pennies?"*

"I would be delighted to do so. . ." came the voice, *"if you can wait a minute."*

—C. Thomas Hilton
(abridged for clarity)

It is part of human nature to want things *Now.* This is but one part of your humanity you will have to learn to suppress before you can succeed.

The casino will be working against you in this regard, but you must not stray. Of all the clubs in your golf bag, *patience* is the one you will need the most.

Before you can learn to *Win*, you must learn how to *Not Lose.* The latter is far more important, for the casino will use every device at its disposal (and they have many) to ensure that you lose as big as the Eagle Nebula.

If you learn only one thing today, learn this: *Discipline is all that separates you from the losers and the fools.*

Take the shortcut, and learn this *Now.*

THE HOUSE EDGE DEFINED

Before moving on, we're going to have to take a look at that statistical vampire known as the *house edge*. This is one concept you should understand inside and out, because it's what guarantees the casinos a winning position.

House Edge is the mathematical advantage casinos hold over players, by paying off winning bets for less than what would be paid to fairly compensate the risk that's involved. You see, there is a precise statistical probability for every bet you can make in a casino. If you were paid the exact inverse of a bet's probability every time, in theory neither you nor the casino would ever win. Both of you would just be turning over money, with no hope of long-range gain.

The house edge is the unseen foe that never sleeps. It works against you with every bet you make, grinding away your fortunes with persistent malicious intent.

To illustrate, we'll look at the game of roulette. This game has thirty-eight numbers on the layout: 1 through 36, plus 0 and 00. If you place a bet on one of these numbers, you'll be paid 35 to 1 for every winning bet. But wait a minute. There's only one chance in 38 that you'll win, according to its statistical probability. So, you're paid 35 to 1 for taking a 37 to 1 risk.

The difference is the house edge.

At American roulette, that edge is 5.26%, which means the casino earns an average of $5.26 out of every $100 wagered, by virtue of that statistical advantage.

All games are structured to guarantee the house a favorable position in this way. But despair not. Ahead, you will learn of its antidote, the *Player's Edge*.

THE DAGWOOD EDGE

I can't believe we had to go all the way to five out of nine.

—Dagwood Bumstead

FIGURE 1
The Dagwood Edge

Now that we've discussed the *House Edge,* let's take a look at the *Dagwood Edge.*

In Figure 1 above, Dagwood has opted to let a coin toss decide whether he will take a nap or give Daisy a bath. He wants to give each side a fair chance, but prefers one outcome over the other. How does he get what he wants? He keeps tossing the coin until the desired side wins a majority.

That, my friends, is the Dagwood Edge: *keep the game moving until the preferred side wins.* This is a simplified version of the *player's edge,* and its effectiveness would be hindered in real life by the *house edge,* but it helps make a point: *You* have the capacity to think, react, stay in the game or leave. A gaming table can't maneuver or react. It is reacted *upon.* The player, not the table, has the final say.

2

THE CASINO'S POINT OF VIEW

Those houses weren't built by giving money away.

—Dale Rabiner,
financial consultant

In any competitive situation, it is important to understand the strengths and weaknesses of your adversary. What is the worst he can do to you? What is the worst you can do to him? Like any capable general in a wartime situation, you should be prepared for the full spectrum of strategic possibilities.

This applies especially in gaming, for your opponent has accumulated a track record that is worthy of deep admiration. One can learn from that kind of success.

It would most definitely be advantageous for you to learn to *think like a casino,* if only for the length of time it takes for you to grasp the logic applied therein.

Have you ever thought about the lengths to which casinos go to create an attractive, appealing destination? It seems that no expense is spared to create an environment that is the ultimate in hospitality, party atmosphere and glitter, wrapped around the charming illusion that you can get rich quick while living it up in a lifestyle of decadence and gluttony.

A number of existing casinos cost over $1 billion to build. How do they pay for all that atmosphere?

The atmosphere, though, mustn't hinder the flow of dollars. Atlantic City casinos have no windows in the gaming area on the walls that would otherwise afford an ocean view. They want you to be undistracted when the money is flowing. That's why you won't see a clock from where you sit at a table game, and it's why some casinos pump fresh oxygen into the gaming area. The free drinks help loosen the players' grips on their wallets, and the tokens used at the table games play down the importance of all that money you're putting at risk.

All this is calculated to trigger your compulsive nature. Over the years it has been refined to a science. And yet, after all that, the casinos would be content to win just a fifty-dollar profit from each player. Unlike most of their guests, they appreciate the power of the small return.

Now, you must realize that the casino has a huge advantage over the individual player, for the small return *they* get is multiplied times the thousands of guests that pass through their doors each day. But how many of these guests would be content with that same fifty-dollar win?

It is *greed* that destroys the players, and keeps all the casinos profitable.

Steve Wynn, builder of some of the most successful casinos in the world, including the Mirage, Bellagio, Golden Nugget and Treasure Island, was once quoted as saying that *the best way to make money in a casino is to own one.* Well. Not much point in arguing with that, but this book is for those who lack the $400 million to build their own. The next best thing is to become a *table game specialist,* and put your money at risk in much the same way as a casino.

The weapons casinos use to close the sale and guarantee their income are known as *Compulsion, Continuum* and *House Edge.* Before you go out there to challenge the giant, you should know about the weapons in its arsenal, and especially, their psychological effects on you, the player.

COMPULSION:
THE ENEMY WITHIN

Remember, the House doesn't beat a player. It merely gives him the opportunity to beat himself.

—Nick "The Greek" Dandalos

Compulsion is defined in the American Heritage dictionary as *an irresistible impulse to act, regardless the rationality of the motivation.*

The above definition has been abridged to reflect only the part that is relevant for this context. In casino gambling, it describes those less-than-noble personality traits the casinos will attempt to coax out of you: hedonism and greed.

Compulsion is a treacherous adversary, because to fight it is to fight your natural inclinations. Even seasoned professionals can succumb to this beast, for although they have learned to suppress it, it's always beckoning from the shadows.

When losing, it is natural to find yourself edging toward a state of panic. How are you going to absorb the losses you just incurred? You're hurt and confused, because someone just took your money away. How are you going to get it back?

Maybe now (after eight consecutive losses) is the time to *load up* and get back everything you lost with one large, well-timed bet.

Sounds like a plan!

This is what goes through one's mind. It's part of being human. The casinos know it. They wait for it. It's the reason for their success. Watching their guests self-destruct before their very eyes is part of their daily routine.

For those readers who wish to hear the outcome of that large, well-timed bet, there are three possibilities:

1) The player reached into his pocket but realized he was tapped out. The (planned) bet was never made.

2) He lost that bet also, bringing his string of losses to nine. Don't think it can't happen to you.

3) He won, and was thrilled until his next crisis, when he tried it again, and lost big. Spelled: B-I-G.

If you're thinking result number three could have worked out, no, no, no. Winning a bet conceived through one's sur-render to compulsion only validates the habit, which will inevitably lead to severe consequences down the road.

Compulsion works against you when you're winning, too. When things are going well at the tables, one tends to feel invincible. This is your big moment. As the dice fly across the table, you imagine the headlines: "Local man makes thirty-five passes at the craps table, shattering all records!" This is the chance of a lifetime. You pick up the dice and run through the list of ways to tell your idiot boss he can take that job and shove it. You'll never have to put up with his black-hearted, self-righteous, ritualistic power trips again!

Oops. You just heard the words "Seven out, line away, eight was," and poof. . .the dream is gone.

Jeez, you were doing so well. You couldn't even make an easy point like the eight?!

Oh well. It was a beautiful dream while it lasted.

Now: if you can figure a way to avoid losing *and* winning while at the tables, compulsion won't be a problem.

CONTINUUM:
THE UNBROKEN CHAIN

The applicable definition of *"continuum"* is *a continuous extent or succession that has no arbitrary division.*

Casino games move fast. Decision after decision occurs and the action never stops. You may have just won a thousand with a bet at the craps table, but you have no time to savor that victory or plan your next move, for the dice never stop rolling. Do you give up your place at the table, or try to stall for time? This is *Continuum:* an absence of time to react to the never-ending succession of betting opportunities.

What about the players making smaller bets? They also fall victim because they stay too long. Within minutes, they lose the ability to keep pace with the table, and seldom have the sense to quit after that big score, *if* it ever comes.

My craps sessions usually last thirty to forty minutes. In that time I often see a lot of players come and go. Some of them hang on tenaciously, but too many, I think, have acquired the nasty habit of playing right down to their last chip.

Compulsion and *House Edge* also did their dirty work, but *Continuum* was the key player. The repetition and monotony of ongoing play pulled them in and turned them all into reckless, irresponsible, mechanical robots that moved without thinking. *That* is the hypnotic effect of that unconscionable foe known (only in this book) as *Continuum.*

HOUSE EDGE: THE STATISTICAL ADVANTAGE

Fear makes the wolf bigger than he is.

—*God's Little Instruction Book*

Meet the casino's most notorious weapon: the house edge. This is what guarantees its profits. In theory, as long as the casino keeps the games moving it can do nothing but win, for the numbers will automatically fall in its favor.

That's all it takes to make a successful business.

In Nevada, some casinos advertise a 98% return on their slot machines. What does that mean? Well, for every dollar taken in, an average of 98 cents is returned to the player. How do they make money? Volume. If a casino's take from its slots is five million dollars a day, it will net $100,000. Not a bad day's pay for a game that doesn't even require a dealer.

Figure 2 shows the Statistical Casino Advantage for games found in most casinos. These are arranged in order, with the best deals for the player at the top of the list.

For all its notoriety, house edge is the least destructive of the three mentioned in this section. The craps player who lost $200 in twenty minutes didn't do so because of the house edge. There are bigger demons out there.

If you stick to the bets recommended in this book, you shouldn't have to worry (too much) about the residual damage arising from the house edge.

STATISTICAL CASINO ADVANTAGE

GAME / BET	HOUSE EDGE
CRAPS: Pass or Don't Pass with double odds	0.60%
Pass or Don't Pass with single odds	0.80%
Patrick System, Pass/Don't Pass	0.92%
MINI-BACCARAT: (betting on) Bank	1.17%
(betting on) Player	1.36%
EUROPEAN ROULETTE with *En Prison:* Even money bets	1.35%
CRAPS: Pass Line or Don't Pass (only)	1.41%
CRAPS: Place bet on the 6 or 8	1.52%
ATLANTIC CITY ROULETTE: Even money bets	2.63%
CRAPS: Place bet on 5 or 9	4.00%
Buy bet on 4 or 10	5.00%
Lay bets (Any number)	5.00%
AMERICAN ROULETTE: All bets except Fiveline	5.26%
CRAPS: Place bet on 4 or 10	6.67%
AMERICAN ROULETTE: Fiveline bet	7.89%
CRAPS: Hardway 6 or 8	9.09%
Hardway 4 or 10	11.11%
Any Craps	11.11%
Any Seven (Big Red)	16.67%
MONEY WHEEL: All bets	11.00% & up
HORSE RACING: All bets	15.00% & up
KENO: All bets	22.00% & up

FIGURE 2

WHAT ODDS MEAN AND HOW THEY'RE FIGURED

In this business, you won't last ten minutes if you're not clear on this business of *Odds:* what they mean, why they change, and their monetary significance.

No place—I imagine—are odds more closely watched than at thoroughbred racetracks, where you will find Pari-Mutuel odds, which are determined by the bettors as a group. The mystique and allure of the ever-changing odds, in fact, figures prominently in the success of thoroughbred racing as a business. So this is where we will look for definition.

Figure 3 shows the range of odds commonly seen at racetracks. These prices show the return for a basic $2.00 bet. According to the chart, a winning 1–1 bet pays $4. Two dollars of that figure is your original wager; the other two represent your profit, which in effect works out to a 100% return on your investment.

So how are odds figured? It's easy once you understand it. From Figure 3, you can see that a 5–2 bet pays $7.00. For any odds, divide the second number into the first (resulting in the odds for each dollar wagered), then multiply it times two (since the minimum racetrack bet is two dollars), then add the return of your basic two-dollar bet. Accordingly, the math for a 5–2 wager would be:

$$5 \div 2 = 2\tfrac{1}{2} \times 2 = 5 + 2 = 7 \text{ dollars.}$$

This isn't as complicated as it appears, and once you know it, you can apply it to all odds and to multiples thereof.

APPROXIMATE ODDS

Return on a successful $2.00 wager

1-9 PAYS $2.20	8-5 PAYS $5.20	7-1 PAYS $16.00
1-5 PAYS $2.40	9-5 PAYS $5.60	8-1 PAYS $18.00
2-5 PAYS $2.80	2-1 PAYS $6.00	9-1 PAYS $20.00
1-2 PAYS $3.00	5-2 PAYS $7.00	10-1 PAYS $22.00
3-5 PAYS $3.20	3-1 PAYS $8.00	15-1 PAYS $32.00
4-5 PAYS $3.60	7-2 PAYS $9.00	20-1 PAYS $42.00
1-1 PAYS $4.00	4-1 PAYS $10.00	30-1 PAYS $62.00
6-5 PAYS $4.40	9-2 PAYS $11.00	40-1 PAYS $82.00
7-5 PAYS $4.80	5-1 PAYS $12.00	50-1 PAYS $102.00
3-2 PAYS $5.00	6-1 PAYS $14.00	99-1 PAYS $200.00

FIGURE 3

The reason Figure 3 is entitled *Approximate Odds* is that all racetrack odds fall within a range. If the final odds for a winning horse reads 5–2, for example, it will pay no less than $7.00, and as much as $7.80 (for every $2 bet), in increments of 20 cents. That's five different prices you could get from a successful bet (to Win) on a horse with 5–2 odds.

Racetracks do it this way for two reasons: simplicity and breakage. The simplicity is to avoid the confusion that would occur if the track posted hundreds of different odds figures, and breakage refers to the slice the track pays itself when rounding downward to the next 10- or 20-cent increment as the payouts are tallied.

Racetrack odds are more precise than casino odds, which is why they were chosen to illustrate the concept. In a casino, a $2.00 bet on anything with 2–1 odds (for example) returns exactly $6.00. Not a penny more or a penny less.

As a final word, it is important to distinguish between casino odds of say, 8 *to* 1 and 8 *for* 1. The former returns 8 units profit for each unit wagered, plus the return of your original bet. The latter gives you 8 units for 1, period. Translated, 8 *for* 1 equals 7 *to* 1. Why are there two methods? For the same reason a $3.00 burger is priced $2.99.

SUMMARY: COMPULSION, CONTINUUM, AND HOUSE EDGE

Compulsion, Continuum and *House Edge* comprise the essence of the casino's arsenal, and should be feared in that order. In the absence of these three, casinos might need federal aid to thrive in our society.

The best way to handle *Compulsion* is to keep tabs on what you're doing, as if you're watching yourself. When you begin to deviate from the plan, it's time to bail out. Do so quickly before you get mangled and mauled!

Continuum is manageable as long as you make it a point to pace yourself, and, not stay too long. Don't let the table put you in a trance. Stay on top of things.

Obviously, you should stick to the bets that carry the lower house percentages, for although *house edge* is characterized as being the least harmful of the three, there lies the accompanying presumption that you have the good sense to avoid (as a general rule, but not as an absolute) those bets that carry percentages running into two figures.

The best way to avoid all three of these trappings is to make it a habit to keep your visits to the casinos as brief as possible, and, watch yourself like a hawk. You're part of a commando mission, raiding an enemy target. You need to strike quickly and deep, then get on out of there.

The ones who lose are the ones who stay too long.

3

FUNDAMENTALS
OF GAMING

If you have built castles in the air, your work need not be lost. That is where they should be. Now put the foundations under them.

—Henry David Thoreau

Knowing what to expect of one's opponent is what separates the winner from the loser. Especially, when gambling in a casino, the better you understand common table trends, the better you can coordinate your game plan.

The key to successful gambling lies in the ability to anticipate trend development. You need to size up the table as you play, and chart a course in your mind that represents its logical destination. Then you act on that projection—for as long as you can continue to win.

If you don't get this; if this concept escapes you, I don't guess there's much of a future for you in this area. Trends are what bring on the wins. Love trends as you love life itself, for they are your roadmap, when you're seeking your way along the dark and thorny path to success.

They will mislead you at times. But once you understand them, they will be your friend.

TRENDS IN GAMING

*There are things we don't understand, yet they exist none-
theless.*

—Lt. Worf, from
Star Trek, The Next Generation

It is said to be proven that the house will win in the long
run. Against the crowd, this is true. But an accomplished player
knows that *trends are more powerful than statistical imperatives.*
If this was not the case, it's not likely that career gambling would
exist in any form on planet earth.

Trends are the positive and negative aspects of the game.
Any game. They represent the highs and the lows. To a seasoned
player, they offer direction.

Back in the days when I believed in fighting the trend, I
once made the twelve-hour trip to Atlantic City, parked the car,
and headed straight for the roulette pit at Trump Plaza. At one of
the tables, I watched as black came up six times in a row.
Definitely, that table was ripe for a bet on red. Hell, it was
overdue. By my way of seeing things at the time, this was a gift.

My $10 wager lost when black appeared again, so on the
next spin I bet $20 on red. I was brimming with overconfidence
as I watched the little white ball circle the wheel. But it landed
on another black number. Strangely, I was gaining confidence as
I put down $50 on the next spin, but black won yet again. Time
to bring out the cannon. I laid a $100 bill on the table and said to
the dealer, *"One black, on red."* In about a minute, I watched as
my bet sunk like a stone, loss number four.

Well. This had to be a historical first. And I was there to see it happen. Surely this is front page stuff. But where's the reporter? Where's the camera crew?

There was only one other player at the table, a young lad who had been putting a $5 chip on black with every spin. *What a loser,* I thought, not quite getting the point that he had been winning the whole time.

Hesitating a little, the 'loser' put yet another chip on black. Is he nuts? Does he expect black to win *again,* after ten straight? *I'll* show him how it's done.

With the confidence of a man who'd seen the future and knew the result, I put $200 on red.

It was a long ride home.

My trip allotment was $400, and $380 of that was gone in six minutes, speculating on red to win just one time. Later, I learned that streaks of eleven are not that uncommon.

That was the hardway lesson in trends. Hopefully, you'll learn something from what you've just read.

There's a saying that is the law of the land for horseplayers: Once you spot a pattern, it's gone. This is true for most players, because they're unable to see the big picture. They're looking for trends that are localized and immediate. They miss the larger portrait that is painted right in front of them.

In this line, you will frequently encounter what appear to be historical firsts; things you would not have thought possible had you not seen them with your own eyes. In time, you'll become inured to the incredible, and you'll expect the unexpected.

When an aberration occurs at the tables, don't run and hide. Chase it down. Take it for all its worth, for this is one way you win in the casinos. Just don't use that as an excuse to abandon your discipline, for that is how you *lose* in casinos.

Gambling is a tricky business.

Though these things defy one's imagination, they've always occurred and always will, as long as man and casino games endure. I call it the *defiance of rational explanation.* But there's a logical reason for every bit of it. . . .

THE RANDOM WALK

*Chance is always powerful; let your hook always be cast.
In the pool where you least expect it, there will be a fish.*
—Ovid

The concept of the Random Walk was introduced about three hundred years ago, and has been studied by some of the greatest men of modern science, including Albert Einstein. For brevity, we'll cover only the basic concept.

We will use the flip of a coin to illustrate the point. If you are standing in one place, and have decided to move one step to the right after every heads decision, and one to the left after tails, where will you be after, say, twenty decisions?

Most of the time, you'll end up close to where you started, but if you keep repeating the same trial, there will be times when one side may win fifteen out of twenty, for example, which would put you way to the left, or way right.

If you persist, you'll get results that are even farther out, but as you do so, the totals for all decisions from each side will move closer to 50%. This is known as the Law of Very Large Numbers. There are books currently in print (that address the scientific aspects of random numerical events) that show the bell curve that is formed by such cumulative trials.

Now, stop and think for a moment about the ongoing action in your average casino. At a craps table, the dice may roll 200 times an hour. Multiply that times 24 hours and then that result times an average of three active tables. That works out to 14,400 betting opportunities a day, just for the game of craps.

On that basis, with betting from all other table games added in, Trump Plaza in Atlantic City (for example) may well produce over 100,000 table game results every day.

From those 100,000 decisions, there will be a percentage that is skewed to the outer limits—when viewed in groups—and another percentage that isn't quite so far out but is nonetheless unique. Most of the time you'll get your even balance per the experiment. But keep in mind: while some tables are doing *this,* others are doing *that,* resulting in the occurrence of numerous 'outer limit trends' at almost any point in time, in any active casino.

The seasoned player knows that all he has to do is play the games, and the trends will come to him. They're part of the natural order of things, especially in casinos, where trends live and grow in abundance. And some players (like myself) make it a point to look for specific trends, allowing one to (occasionally) bet with pinpoint precision. At a craps table, there are numerous outward signs that tell you whether the dice are likely to pass. At a roulette table, the scoresigns (used by the major casinos) tell you right up front what's going on at that table, and what's *been* going on for the last twenty decisions or so.

When you start to understand the dominion of trends, your outlook will change, and your game will improve.

TRENDS IN EVERYDAY LIFE

It may help you to understand trends in gaming if you are reminded that they are part of everyday living. People seldom think about it, but trends can in fact influence or even alter the direction of one's personal development.

Surely you've had days when everything went wrong, and then days when things went superbly. This is a truly remarkable trend, because it is not confined to a single category; it affects all that you do and everything you touch for an entire day!

Have you ever tried to buy an item that you don't often use, and can't find a store that has it in stock, anywhere in the city? Have you ever run an errand, and all fifteen traffic lights you had to pass through were green? Have you ever gone weeks without a date, then have two the same night? Or noticed that both of the local college basketball teams won last night's game by exactly fourteen points? Or after listening to an hour of junk on the radio, suddenly they're playing all your favorite songs?

Maybe you haven't seen or experienced any of this, but I think most people can relate to the concept.

You need to be aware of the existence of trends, because it helps you avoid being thrown off balance by a statistical fluke that may occur when your money is on the line: *Did you see that? The 12 came up four out of the last five rolls!* So what? You can't let that throw you off your game.

If you pursue gaming as more than just a lark, expect to be floored on a regular basis by trends that defy your imagination, and all manner of explanation!

A FIRE WHICH NEVER DIES

Mozart: *How would you translate that?*
Salieri: *Consigned to flames of wall.*
Mozart: *Do you believe in it?*
Salieri: *In what?*
Mozart: *A fire which never dies, burning you forever.*
Salieri: *(pause) Oh, yes.*
—from the movie *Amadeus*

There was once an experiment I performed in Atlantic City: I went from casino to casino, looking for a craps table that showed outward signs of warmth. At the appropriate moment, I played one $25 bet and then moved on to another table or casino. Betting on that basis, I won eleven out of fifteen wagers. The next day I tried the exact same thing, but encountered results that were radically different. (I quit for the day after losing six out of six bets.)

Those examples demonstrate the power of trends, for though my betting activity was not confined to a single casino, the trend was consistent, offering winners on the one day, then reversing its course on the following day. It reminded me of the fire which never dies, as quoted above.

Moving from table to table can help one reduce the damage inflicted by the house edge, but keep your eye on the big picture. If losses begin to mount, *change the procedure to concur with the results the tables are disposed to give.* But in doing so, react *to the group,* not just the latest result.

You cannot win against the fire which never dies.

THE CLUSTER PRINCIPLE

FIGURE 4
Fourteen events, evenly spaced

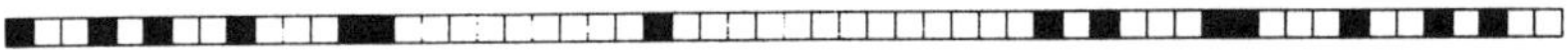

FIGURE 5
Fourteen events, randomly spaced

Through the years, people ask: *How can anyone hope to beat the house when the games are slanted in their favor?*

The need to provide a concise answer forced me to examine what I've been doing, which led to the definition of a targeting method for wagering that I call the *Cluster Principle.*

Figure 4 shows fourteen events, *evenly spaced* along a lateral continuum of fifty-six trials. If gaming events were assembly lines, the black squares would represent a one in four chance, meriting a 3–1 return to equitably compensate the risk.

Below it, Figure 5 shows fourteen events *randomly spaced* along the same continuum. This figure more closely illustrates authentic table game results.

Take a good look at Fig. 5. In the middle of the continuum there are two large gaps. Then look at the impact of those gaps on the other results. Because of the extended absence of that event, (which will frequently occur), the remaining results are compressed into tight groups, or clusters.

Now, in real life, it's not likely that Figure 5's dry spell would self-correct (so as to concur with the probability) by the fifty-sixth result, but this helps illustrate the *Cluster Principle:*

For every absence of a probable event, there is an equivalent compression of subsequent events.

This is kind of like saying that *what goes up must come down.* If, for example, an event that has a one-in-four expectation does not occur for one hundred decisions. . .somewhere, a deficit is accruing. Now, we all know the dice and the roulette wheel have no memory, but the fact remains: statistically, a deficit is mounting, and at some point that debt will have to be paid. The Law of Averages cannot be defied forever.

How do players win when the games are slanted toward the casino? They target the clusters. They wait until the table sends a signal revealing what it's likely to do next, then make their play. That is, after all, why they came.

What does this tell you? Well, if an event isn't happening, don't chase it. Bet on it after it begins to show up and lay back when it fades. You won't catch a 'cluster' every time, but if you make it a habit to wait for the right signals, you won't spend so much time chasing rainbows in the dark.

POSITIVE AND NEGATIVE TRENDS

In gaming, all table patterns can be classified as belonging to one of the following groups:

1) *Positive Trends:* Events that occur in clusters.
2) *Negative Trends:* Prolonged absences of an event.
3) *Neutral Table Patterns:* Ordinary event sequences.

These were just covered, but they hadn't been given names. Each one could be exploited in gaming situations, though most serious players prefer *positive* trends. Then again, some do favor the *negative* trends. And ahead, you will learn of procedures designed for the *neutrals* (ordinary event sequences).

Positive trends refer to the presence of an event, in groups or in clusters. Negative trends describe the absence of an event. Neutrals are normal, uneventful table patterns.

Positive trends are generally more fruitful than negatives, because the aberration favors the event instead of opposing it. The problem is, a positive trend may have run its course by the time its presence is realized. This is why it's important to try to anticipate trend development at the tables.

This book advocates the pursuit of positive trends, because chasing negative trends is, in effect, fighting the trend.

If you specialize in certain table patterns or events, positive trends will be easier to catch in the early stages, for you'll be waiting for their arrival. The trap will be set.

SUMMARY OF TRENDS IN GAMING

Some years ago, I remember saying to someone, *"When you understand numbers, you understand life."* That may have just been some trash I was talking; I don't know. But I think the same could be said for trends, though doing so will probably help you understand gaming, more than life.

Trends, believe it or not, can help you see into the future. Such a vision is far from definite, but frequently solid enough to justify a wager.

For me to suggest that positive and negative trends are both bettable situations may seem like a contradiction. But you see, both represent a deviation from the norm. This is when you must pay attention to subsequent developments, for they often herald the arrival of a new table direction.

Some gaming authors don't say a word about trends, while others leave it to the reader to decide their importance. And I say that you cannot hope to succeed until you understand them, for they are at the heart of successful gambling.

Life's a gamble. Whenever you run a yellow light, put your moves on a babe or drink city tap water, you're just rolling the dice. There's a measure of risk in everything you do.

As long as you're doing all that gambling, you might as well make it pay. In today's world, your chances for success increase in direct proportion to how well you know the odds, and understand the power of trends.

4

THE GARDEN OF RISK

To win, you have to risk loss.
—Jean-Claude Killy

It was the movie *Cocoon* that taught me a very memorable lesson about the polarity between *yin* and *yang*. In that movie, a group of extraterrestials had been using a swimming pool to store embryonic aliens. Some senior citizens were using that pool on the sly, and had noticed that the water gave them incredible vitality. But while they were gaining energy, the aliens in the cocoons (under the water) were being robbed of their lives.

Initially, the seniors thought they had discovered a fountain of youth. But the real world isn't like that, is it? When someone gains, someone will lose. Whenever you push a button *down,* somewhere, another button is going to pop *up.*

So it is when you live in the *Garden of Risk.* Even if you are lucky enough to win, you cannot continue to do so with impunity, because your wins are causing somebody else to lose. And trust me on this: nobody likes to lose.

They say discretion is the better part of valor. It is also one of the unspoken precepts of the *Player's Edge.*

THE PLAYER'S EDGE

Neglect not the gift that is in thee.

—New Testament
I Timothy 4:14

As if a counterweight to the knowledge that your opponent is indomitable, it's a good feeling to walk into a casino and know that *you* have the edge. A successful gambler—by definition—*has* to win more than lose. . .but exactly what are the contents of his little bag of tricks?

The *Player's Edge* consists of four points:

1) *When losing, you can walk.*
2) *You can vary the size of your wagers.*
3) *You can choose where to play.*
4) *You can respond to the table results.*

Most people don't know what an advantage these offer. In effect, the casino is confined to linear movement while you can move in any direction you please. To elaborate:

1) *When losing, you can walk.* Casinos don't have this option. Can you imagine being stripped to the bone by a mob of greedy players while you stand there, powerless to stop them? Casinos face this dilemma every time a craps table heats up, or some high rollers get lucky at baccarat. There's not much the casino can do—except go to the vault.

2) *You can vary the size of your bet.* Ideally, a player should bet low or leave when losing, and press up his bets when winning. It's called lose low, win high. It's how you minimize losses and maximize your gains.

3) *You can choose where to play.* Frequently, there are signs that clue you in to the table's temperature or disposition. Some tables whisper and some shout. Of course, you never know what the future will bring at any given table, but you're better off if you make it a habit to be selective.

Also, you can take your business to where the best deals are. Not all casinos make the same payoffs for bets. Some pay 14–1 for the 3 or 11 at craps; others offer 15–1. Some pay triple for a field roll 12 while most pay double. Some don't charge the house commission unless you win; most of them do.

4) *You can react and respond to the table results.* Every table you will encounter is inanimate. It may seem otherwise, but the truth is, it does not think. *You* can adjust to the changing situation as the changes occur. *You* can bob and weave, thrust and parry, circle and pounce. The table can't react to anything. It just grinds out numbers, endlessly and forever. It is doomed to a life of being reacted *upon.*

Imagine that it had a life of its own. Imagine that it could fight back. For just a moment, imagine.

The *Player's Edge* is the sum of the points listed above, plus this very pertinent advice: *Be discreet about your wins and losses.* You can't afford to let the world know how much money you're turning over, because 1) there are people out there who would kill you for fifty bucks, and 2) the casinos can deny you access, if you prove to be a continuous drain on their resources. If you seek a long and prosperous life on planet earth, it may serve your interests to keep these in mind.

The end goal of the *player's edge* is to neutralize the destructive effects of the *house edge.* But your biggest 'edge' is sourced to your discipline. The same kind of discipline, in fact, the casinos expect from their obedient staff!

THE COLDEST GAME

There is no law that says you cannot lose 100 consecutive bets.

—the Author

It may serve you to recite the words above, or commit them to memory. Now, I'm sure that no player ever lost that many, because he'd be BROKE long before he even got close. But fate and chance work in mysterious ways.

To illustrate the point, let me tell you about a trip of mine to Las Vegas some years ago. One of my first buy-ins was at a craps table at the Mirage. I was playing a variation of following the (line bet) trend, where I would switch to the opposite of what I was doing after three consecutive losses. I ended up leaving after losing twelve straight bets.

You can't imagine how that felt. Losing $250 was nothing. What got to me was battling a force that could read my thoughts and cause the opposite result of my bet, every single time. You see, I was changing my tactics after every three losses, but old *Mister Opposite* kept pace with every step.

Granted, twelve losses is far from a hundred, but you know, I never saw the end of that streak. If you put yourself in that place, you might understand that it seemed like something from the *Twilight Zone.* But there's no reason the table can't do the opposite of what you do, indefinitely.

At the time, it didn't occur to me that this was the polar opposite of what had worked so well in Atlantic City, playing the same strategy. It's not so strange when you win!

It is this type of situation that separates discipline in gaming from that which is needed in other areas of expertise. You've got to take these aberrations in stride, as the casinos do. It's either that, or go down in flames.

It's always amusing to see the house lose. Once, at the Sands in Atlantic City, I held the dice for forty minutes. The other players at the table were cross-eyed with delight, since some of them made thousands from my roll. I was wondering when the boxman would complain that I was throwing the dice wrong, or get nasty in an attempt to shut me down. How was he going to explain the $40,000 hit that occurred on his watch?

He never said a word. He just sat there smiling, as if he was enjoying every minute of *our* enjoyment. He knows that you've got to take the bad with the good, but more importantly, he knows that in the long run, the casino will do nothing but win. This reminded me how important it is to *think like a casino* when things start to go south.

You will never have to worry about being held hostage in a situation like that, while your opponents grow rich before your eyes. You'll walk at the first sign of trouble. But it can't be done without discipline.

Well then, exactly what is discipline? In the simplest terms, it is a combination of patience, restraint and seasoning. It is the recognition that it's far easier to lose than to win, and the ability, when necessary, to suppress your basic human instincts. It is an unwavering commitment to stay the course and remain oblivious to all the temptations that surround you every minute of the day. And it's the coldest game you'll ever play.

One of the things that held me back for a good many years was misunderstanding the concept. I would ask myself: what is the disciplined move to make in this situation?

Don't give it a thought. This book spells out precisely what you should do. All you have to do is stay on track and follow the procedure.

The wins will come.

A PREVIEW

If you don't win, you're a goat.

—Jon David Sherry

What is life like, for those who gamble for a living? Is it at all like the glamorous image of gamblers frequently propagated by Hollywood? Or are those who gamble consigned to a life of frustration, despair, and of forever missing the point that they can never beat the house, as non-gamblers believe?

There is a Yugoslav proverb that goes *Nine gamblers could not feed a single rooster.* And I have to say that in most cases, that would be true. Does that clarify the picture?

There exist, however, a select few who possess a rare blend of qualities, that enables them to consistently succeed. Ironically, they hate to gamble. Putting large sums of money at risk every day scares them half to death. But the day they stop being afraid is the day they go down with a deafening crash.

Some of these individuals live a good life. But they can never truly relax and set the machine on cruise, because all that they've worked so hard to gain can be lost, as quick as a wink. Nor will they ever get a promotion, recognition from their peers, or an award for outstanding achievements. And it's hard to enjoy a fine meal when you know that you're just moments away from setting foot in the lion's den.

But what is this life really like? The following is a picture of how it could be, under the best of circumstances.

One thing you should know, is that even for a seasoned player, there is no such thing as a sure bet. The closest you will come is what this book calls an educated bet. But in such a case, you never, ever *bet the farm* no matter how good the odds are. Even if the game is stacked mightily in your favor, it's a bad bet if it compels you to overextend yourself.

You don't need to rely on lucky wins. There's no reason for you to take that kind of chance when you have the skill to do well without taking heavy risks.

One of the paradoxes of gaming is how you will feel when you enter a casino as an accomplished player. Part of you feels a sense of pride that you can withdraw money from the casinos as if they were banks holding cash reserves in your name. But another part will feel weak and inadequate because once again you've got to put your money at risk, and the very thought makes you a little sick to your stomach. Yesterday, you were right more times than not, just as you were last week, month and year. But today, the counter has been reset to 000, and you have to start all over, building the day's empire from scratch. And who are you to presume that you can take on such an opponent, built from the losses of, actually, *millions* of players?

You're a winner, that's who! Your track record shows that you've attained a level of proficiency that few have ever known. You've paid your dues. You know how to exercise restraint in the heat of battle. Your work is interesting, even a bit enjoyable, but you know how to anchor that enjoyment with an awareness of what can go wrong, and how quickly it can happen.

As you stride down the aisles, you shake your head as you watch the players lose themselves in consumptive greed, for it reminds you of your fate, should you disregard the treacherous undercurrents that silently erode their fortunes away.

Some dealers are envious of your abilities. When the floorperson sees where you've chosen to sit, he might replace the dealer just because you happened to sit there. And the cocktail waitress brings you your favorite drink, *pineapple juice, no ice,* without asking.

Your life is good. You awake at nine-thirty and look out the window at the Atlantic Ocean. You listen to the seagulls as you stroll the boardwalk on your way to breakfast at the Showboat buffet, and there's no hurry to go anywhere or do anything. Your workday might be over by noon or it might not start until midnight. Your call. You have complete control over your life and how you spend your time.

Next week you'll go to the Bahamas where you'll earn just a bit less than your average back home, and you'll have lots of time to explore the cays on a sailboat or cruise the island on a motorbike. And next month you'll be traveling to Europe where you'll visit the French casinos at Trouville and Chamonix before heading to the Casino Ruhl De Nice on the Riviera, and then on to the Mirabeau hotel in Monte Carlo.

Is that kind of life truly attainable? For me to say that the chances are not good is an understatement. You have to have the right kind of personality, and work so hard, that you will wonder why did you ever turn into a glutton for punishment!

There are tricks that can help you. One I use is to remember a quote from Donald Trump's first book, The Art of the Deal: *Protect the downside, and the upside will take care of itself.* That, right there, can take you a long way.

Most important: no matter how good you get, never think for a minute that your opponent is no match for you. Better stay humble if survival is one of your priorities.

Balance is the name of the game. Believe in yourself just as you believe in your rival. And if you subscribe to the notion of *wealth without work,* get out now! As the eloquent poet Ralph Waldo Emerson once wrote: *Only shallow men believe in luck.*

5

CRAPS:
RULES OF PLAY

It's not hard to locate the craps tables in any casino; if you hear spontaneous cheering, there's a good chance that one of the craps tables has been blessed with a hot shooter, that winningest of animals that is like a god to the players.

If you want to see the face of *compulsion,* you'll find it first at the craps table. Craps enthusiasts are by nature the loudest and most undisciplined players you'll ever encounter, because the game was specifically designed to ignite the short fuse of player emotion. Your success as a player may depend, in fact, on your ability to rip out that burning fuse before it has a chance to influence your judgement.

Bank craps is played with a pair of dice that are precision ground for uniformity. The shooter throws the dice across a felt-lined table surrounded by a wall. To ensure a random result, the table crew insists that the shooter toss the dice so they bounce off the far wall before coming to a rest. At the top of the wall is an armrest with trays to hold the players' chips.

Many would-be participants seem to be intimidated by the complicated appearance of the layout, but it's not that difficult to learn this interesting, fast-moving game.

CRAPS PERSONNEL

Most craps tables are manned by a crew of four, consisting of a *boxman,* a *stickman* and two *dealers.* This does not include the *floorperson,* the *pit boss* and an auxiliary dealer who works in shift rotation with the other two dealers and the stickman. Please see Figure 6 on the following page.

The *Dealers* each work a side of the table, taking bets from players and making payoffs. Also, they forward the customers' money to the *boxman* during a buy-in.

The *Stickman* stands in the middle of the table on the same side as the players, moving the dice with a long stick that is bent on one end. He calls out the dice results, hawks proposition bets and frequently advises dealers of payoffs.

The *Boxman* is the one seated, usually wearing a suit and tie. He is responsible for selling the tokens, depositing incoming cash, and settling disputes that may arise. He also checks the dice whenever they accidentally go off the layout.

The *Floorperson* is the next one up the chain. He's the one who may take your player's card so that your level and duration of play can be noted by the *Pit Bookkeeper.*

The *Pit Boss* oversees all the tables in the pit, which is the inner area formed by a group of table games. Any matters that can't be resolved by the other personnel are his domain.

During non-peak hours in smaller casinos, you may come across craps tables that are staffed only by a stickman and one dealer, for economy. In such case, the dealer may request that you situate yourself on the side he's working.

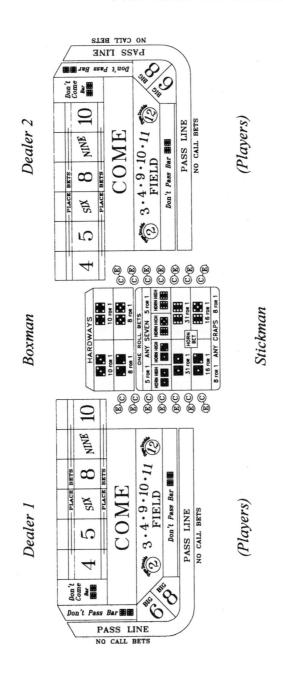

FIGURE 6
Craps Layout

CRAPS TERMINOLOGY

For those of you who are unfamiliar with the terminology used in gaming, there is a glossary of general gaming terms in the back of this book. However, there are a number of terms that apply only to the game of craps, which you should know before we get too deep into the territory.

The *Shooter,* as you have probably guessed, is the one who is rolling the dice.

A *Pass Line* bet is the most popular and basic bet made at the game of craps. It pays even money. A player must put down a pass (or don't pass) bet to qualify as a shooter. The objective of a pass line bettor is to first establish the point, then roll that number one more time before a 7 is rolled.

The *Point* is any one of six numbers: 4, 5, 6, 8, 9 or 10.

The *Come-out* is that period of time between when a shooter first gets the dice and the point number is rolled. (There are five non-point numbers that could be rolled (2, 3, 7, 11 & 12), which can extend the come-out period.

A *Natural* is one of two numbers: 7 or 11, which (if rolled during the come-out) wins instantly for all pass line bettors, and pays even money.

A *Craps* is a 2, 3 or 12, rolled during the come-out. This is the opposite of a natural, for it causes an immediate loss during the come-out for all pass line bettors.

A *Seven-out* is when a 7 is rolled after the point is established, but before the shooter has thrown a repeat of the point number. When this happens, the shooter forfeits the dice to the player to his left, who becomes the new shooter.

A *Don't Pass* bet is basically the reverse image of a pass line bet. Here, you are betting *on* the 7 to be rolled before the point is repeated. And since the 7 is the most frequently rolled number, the odds are that you'll win this bet more often than lose. But there is a serious downside that goes with the package. You lose when a 7 or 11 is rolled during the come-out, which can be responsible for numerous consecutive losses, at times. And it gets worse: the one thing that isn't an exact mirror image of the pass line bet is this little twist: A craps 2, 3 or 12 (which causes a loss to the pass line bettors at the come-out), doesn't necessarily win on the don't side. The numbers 2 and 3 do, but the 12 is a push (a tie with the house). So, during the come-out, the don't pass bettor has six ways to lose instantly (to a natural 7 or 11), three ways to win (from a 2 or 3), and one way (from the 12) to end up with a push.

The *Free Odds* bet (often called *Odds* for simplicity) is one big reason why the pass line bet is so popular. After the point is established, casinos allow you to add a supplemental bet, which pays according to the actual statistical odds for that number to be rolled. This bet pays 2–1 if 4 or 10 is the point; 3–2 for 5 or 9, and 6–5 for the 6 or 8. This is the only bet available in any casino that carries no house edge whatsoever. It is offered as an entice-ment to players, but the catch is that it's not a stand-alone wager; it's only allowed as a tack-on (supplemental) bet to your basic pass or don't pass wager.

Note: On the *right* side (*pass line* betting), playing the *odds* bet is referred to as *taking odds.* On the *wrong* side *(don't pass),* it is called *laying odds.* When you *lay odds,* the return on your bet is not so hot; you get less than even money. Laying odds against the 4 or 10 means betting $40 to win $20 (1–2); on the 5 or 9 you must put up $30 to win $20 (2–3), and for the 6 or 8 it is $24 to win $20 (a 5–6 return).

Lastly, a *Line Bet* is simply a *pass* or *don't pass* wager. This is mentioned only to let you know you can play either one, if the dice are forwarded to you, and the stickman insists that you put down a line bet.

THE CRAPS PROCEDURE

The game commences after a player arrives at a table and makes a buy-in, which involves dropping money on the layout near a dealer, or signing a credit marker. One thing you should know is that the cash must be dropped on the layout; the dealer can't take it from your hand. Also, when buying in, tell the dealer, *"Change only,"* to let him know that you're not trying to place a cash bet on the bet option nearest to where your money landed. After giving the cash to the boxman, the dealer will place your chips on the layout in front of you.

After you receive your chips, you're ready to place some bets. If you are the only player at the table, you have no choice but to be the shooter, else there will be no game. But to qualify as a shooter, you first have to put down a pass or don't pass bet. If there are other players present, however, you can gesture to the effect that you'd like to decline the privilege.

Should you decide to be the shooter, you will select two of the five or six dice that the stickman initially offers, and fling them across the layout so that they bounce against the cushioned end wall that is farthest from where you stand. The stickman will call out the result, then wait for the dealers to pay any bets that may have won on that roll, then push the dice back in front of you with his stick, and you repeat the procedure.

Eventually, you will *seven-out* (roll a 7 during midgame), at which time you forfeit the dice to the player to your left, unless there are no others at the table. If you're alone, you can shoot all night, as long as you've got money.

DICE COMBINATIONS

On the following page, Figure 7 shows the 36 combinations that are possible from a pair of dice. Each number (2 through 12) can be rolled in a finite number of ways. These are the mathematics from which the odds and payoffs are derived in the game of craps.

At the center of the paradigm lies the number 7, which stands taller than the rest. There are six ways this bad boy can be rolled, which makes it the champ. The 6 and 8, which are sister numbers to each other, are the next ones down the chain, then come sister numbers 5 and 9 and so on. Sister numbers are pairs having the same probability. The numbers 6 & 8, 5 & 9, 4 & 10, 3 & 11 and 2 & 12 are all sisters. But there's another reason they are linked: Whatever number appears on the top of a pair of dice is the sister to the number you'll find on the bottom.

To help you understand these probabilities, let us compare the 7 to the 10. According to Figure 7, the 7 can be rolled six ways, and the 10 three ways—out of thirty-six possible ways. Thus, statistically, the 7 is twice as likely to come up as the 10. Which may shed light on why the casinos compensate successful bets on the 10 at a rate close to 2–1: to match the probability, minus a small commission (to cover their expenses). The same figures apply to the sister number of the 10, the 4.

Fighting the seven is what makes this game tough—and interesting. Occasionally the seven will disappear for a while, during which time an aggressive player can reap great rewards. But it's an uphill battle for the players most of the time, which is one reason casinos prosper in our society.

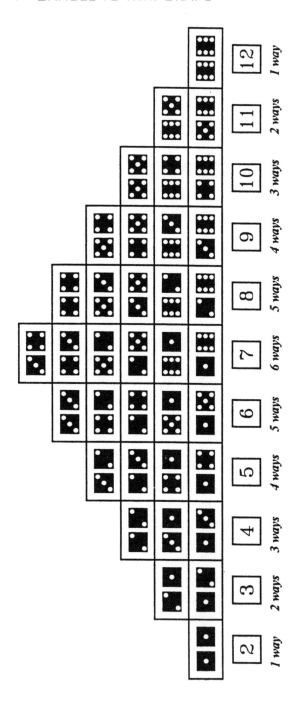

FIGURE 7
Dice Combination Paradigm
(36 Possible ways)

What about playing the other side, where the 7 is your friend? Isn't that the closest you can come to being the house? Perhaps so, but playing *don't pass* is no picnic. Don't forget, the house has a built-in edge no matter which side you pick.

The only way you can beat the casino at its own game is to exploit that which they are powerless to control. *You have to follow the trends* wherever they may lead—on both sides of the game—for as long as they persist.

Inevitably, some readers will have difficulty with one of the aspects of dice combinations. For the number 3, as an example, what's the difference between dice that read 1 & 2, and a reading of 2 & 1? Isn't that just one combination?

It is not. Imagine that one die is red and the other is blue. When 3 is rolled, sometimes the 1 will originate from the red die; other times from the blue. Those are two of the thirty-six possibilities, and all combinations must be accounted for to compute the odds. If the 3 was derived but one way, it would have the same odds as the 2, which has a different probability. And that would throw all the odds and payoffs into a state of gothic disengagement, which may well cause a reactionary breach in the fabric of statistical certainties of the universe.

I'm pretty sure you wouldn't want to be responsible for something like that.

Maybe it'll help if you look at it this way: If a pair of dice was a horse race, the 7 would be the betting favorite, and the 2 & 12 would be the longshots. All the other horses (like dice rolls) would carry odds in between.

WAGERING OPTIONS

PASS LINE: The *pass line* is unquestionably the most popular of all the betting options at craps.

The unshaded portion of Figure 8 shows how the *pass line* would appear on the right side of a craps table. Please note that the bet labeled *Free Odds* is placed right behind the pass line bet. *Free odds* is a bet that can be made as an accompaniment to a *pass line* bet, and it is technically the fairest bet you can make in a casino, for it carries no house edge.

To signify the *point* number, as derived from a dice roll, a *puck* is placed on that number. In this figure, the 4 is the point. After a decision is reached against that number, the puck is flipped over to the OFF side, and placed where shown.

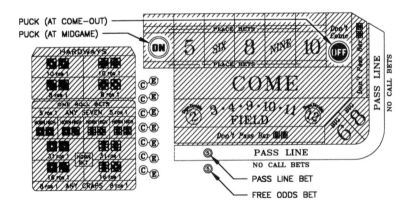

FIGURE 8
The Pass Line

At a typical active craps table, there are six or seven players on each of the two sides, and most, if not all, of the bettors have a bet down on the pass line.

"We're coming out," yells the stickman, pushing the dice to the shooter, who picks them up and throws, say, another four. *"We're out on four,"* the stickman says, as each dealer takes his puck out of the *don't come,* flips it over to the white side *(On),* and places it in the "4" box on the layout. At this point, players at the table add their free odds bet, which they couldn't do until the point (in this case, 4) was established.

Now the *midgame* begins, where some of the bettors put up secondary wagers, called *place* bets, on other numbers. But the fate of the bets now rests in the hands of the shooter. His goal is to roll the four again before the 7, and if he succeeds, the players win along with him. If a 7 comes up first, all pass line bettors lose and the player to his left inherits the dice, and *"comes out"* after the dealers retrieve the losing bets.

As each player *sevens out,* the dice move clockwise around the table to the next player. Any players who don't wish to shoot can indicate so with a hand gesture, in which case the stickman will offer them to the next player.

This is really all there is to the central wager made at craps. The shooter rolls a number, which becomes the point, then tries to roll it again before a 7. He might get a bonus if he rolls a *natural* (7 or 11, which are instant winners during the come-out), or he may get stung by a come-out craps (a 2, 3 or 12, which are instant losers during the come-out). But all he's really trying to do is roll two of the same number, with any amount of other numbers in between, as long as one of them isn't a 7.

The most notable quirk in the rules of this game is that the seven wins during the *come-out,* but loses after the point is established. This is a strong enticement of the game: during the come-out period, pass line bettors have twice as many ways to win instantly (via a *natural* 7 or 11), than lose instantly, by virtue of a *craps* roll of 2, 3 or 12.

DON'T PASS: Near the table with the twelve players betting pass line is another table with four players. The shooter has a bet on pass line, but the others are betting don't pass. After three rolls he sevens out, and shortly, the stickman offers the dice to the next player, who refuses them. So the stickman pushes the dice to the player beyond him, who hesitates, then moves his bet from don't pass to pass, and picks up the dice.

This is a typical don't pass table, known as a *cold table.* Fewer players; everyone betting against the shooter; no one wants to *be* the shooter. Don't pass is the opposite of pass, so when one side wins the other loses. And in that spirit, don't pass bettors are not enthusiastic or abundant.

Most craps tables have no more than one or two don't pass bettors, if any. And sometimes you'll come across an ice-cold table that the bettors refuse to acknowledge: player after player sevens out, but each one thinks he can make the point. That's why the player, two paragraphs back, switched his bet from the *don't pass* to *pass* when the dice came to him. He hesitated because he knew the table was cold, but after a moment's thought, he decided that maybe *he* could change it.

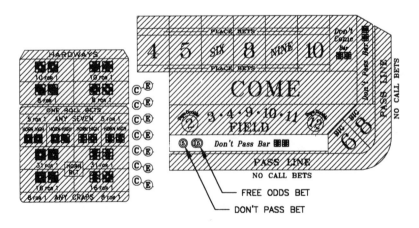

FIGURE 9
The Don't Pass

What about the one who refused the dice? Most players feel that *shooting from the don't* is like betting against oneself. You see, the casino treats only the pass line winners as winners. If you shoot from the don't and make the point, the stickman pronounces it a winner, even though you lost! I think this is done to steer the crowd away from the bets with the best chances to win, but you didn't hear that from me.

When playing the don't, the odds are on your side once the point is established, but getting past the come-out is the trick. The 7 and 11 will kill your bet instantly during the come-out, and there is a much greater chance of that, than for you to win from a *craps* (where only 2 or 3 will win; the 12 is a push). And, there's always the chance you'll get whacked with five straight *naturals,* which can be extremely frustrating.

Most of the time the don't bettor has to endure a tedious grind, for he must settle for low bet returns in exchange for owning a piece of the betting favorite. And when things don't go his way, matters can spiral out of hand with alarming speed, for it may take two wins to compensate a single loss. But then there are times when the dice will go all the way around the table, and no one can make a point. It's times like those that life is good for the don't better; all he's gotta do is ride the wave until it dies, then leave after the first loss.

There are those who specialize in betting the don't; Nick the Greek was a back line player. But such types are usually quiet and withdrawn. They don't want to enrage the pass line bettors, whose *losses* help finance the don't bettor's *wins.*

If not for the extreme risk one faces during the come-out, the don't pass would or should be the number one choice of betting options for those who approach casino gambling as a business. But that come-out can be lethal to those who haven't got the seasoning to weather the storm.

Fortunately, there is a way to take advantage of the superior positioning the don't side offers—without heavy liability. That's coming up ahead.

FREE ODDS FOR PASS LINE: This is the only bet that carries no house edge, but you have to make a line bet to qualify for the privilege.

Understanding the concept of free odds may seem difficult for some, but it's really just three numbers to memorize. We will first look at how free odds apply to pass line bets.

Let's say that as you stroll up to a craps table, a shooter has just made his point. After the dealer finishes paying the winners, you drop $100 on the layout and say *"Change only."* The dealer takes your money and pulls a stack of (twenty) reds from the boxman's chip supply, or he might take them from his own stack. The stickman says *"We're coming out,"* as he pushes the dice back to the shooter. After placing the chips in your rail, you pull one out and drop it in the area marked *pass line* on the layout, directly in front of you.

Your focus is now on the come-out roll. You have eight ways to win (from a 7 or 11) and four ways to lose (via 2, 3 or 12) on the next roll. The odds are in your favor, but there's a greater chance (67%) that your bet won't be immediately affected if the shooter rolls a point number, which he does, a 5.

As the stickman announces *"We're out on 5,"* the players around the table put up their free odds, as shown in Figure 8 (back on page 48). Now, let's hold up a minute.

The *Free Odds* bet is allowed (as a tack-on to a pass line bet) *after* the point is established, and pays according to the statistical probability for that point to be rolled (versus the probability of a 7), as denoted below:

POINT	PROBABILITY	RETURN	$5 PAYS	$10 PAYS
4 or 10	1–2	2–1	$10	$20
5 or 9	2–3	3–2	$6 PAYS $9	$15
6 or 8	5–6	6–5	$6	$12

FIGURE 10
Free Odds for Pass

Figure 10 shows that the probability for the sister numbers of 4 and 10 is 1–2. If 4 was the point, there are three of the thirty-six dice combinations that produce a 4, while the 7 can be rolled 6 ways. The probability is 1–2 because for every (1) way you have to win, there are 2 ways to lose. The house pays 2–1, the inverse of 1–2, to compensate that risk. Moving across the Figure 10 chart, you can see that a $5 bet pays $10 (a 2–1 return), which is your profit, paid alongside the return of your original bet. Therefore, you end up with $15 for every $5 that is wagered on a successful free odds bet against a point of 4.

If a 5 or 9 is the point, the probability that it will be rolled before a 7 is 2–3, so the casino offers a return of 3–2. This is where it gets a little tricky: a 3–2 payoff on a $5 bet would come out to $7.50, and most casinos won't deal in anything except round dollar amounts, at least for bets like this. So they allow [insist on] a $6 *free odds bet* to accompany a $5 *pass line bet,* because a figure divisible by 2 is needed to enable payoffs in even dollar amounts. The $6 bet will return $15, for a $9 profit. (Divisibility is not a problem at the $10 level, for that amount *is* evenly divisible by 2.)

Finally, we come to the 6 and the 8, which have a probability of 5–6, just a hair below even money. For your risk, you get paid 6–5, just a hair above.

Returning to the game we were playing, you were about to put up your free odds against a point of 5. Since your pass line bet is $5, you should put $6 on the other side of the line, or $10 if you wish to take *double odds,* which is permissable in all major casinos. If the shooter rolls a 7 before a 5, both your pass line and odds bet lose, but if instead he rolls a 5, you will win $5 for your pass line bet plus $9 for *(single) odds.* That is your profit, which the dealer sets next to your original bets.

These are good deals. You get your money's worth on all of them, and although you are contesting the seven—which is more probable—there are times when the seven is off duty. This window of opportunity may be small or large, but it's what all right bettors (pass line bettors) look for.

FREE ODDS FOR DON'T PASS: For those times when you want the 7 on your side, *free odds* are available for the don't side as well. The return is always less than even money, but you'll be positioned to win the majority of the time.

The probability and return numbers are the exact inverse of the payoffs one receives when playing the *Do* side. If a house edge was attached to odds bets, the two would not concur.

Notice that the *$5 PAYS* and *$10 PAYS* headings have been replaced with *1x & 2x PAYS.* Since you're now on the reverse side, the constant ($10, as in *$10 PAYS,* for example), is the amount *won* instead of the amount *bet.* And casinos allow you to put up enough money to *win* single or double odds, as a basis for sizing your bet. So, to add double odds to a $5 don't pass bet on the 4, for example, means putting up $20 to win $10.

True, it's a lousy return, but this is what the house pays *you* when you win a *pass line* odds bet on the 4 or 10!

For the other numbers (5, 6, 8 & 9) the penalty is not so huge, but the compensating factor is that those bets won't win as often. All the same, it's nice knowing the 7 is on *your* side.

The only flaw in this bet is that your don't wager must first make it past the come-out for you to be able to win from a 7. And, since the *craps* number 12 doesn't win at the come-out (the lone exception to the perfect inversion), you have only three ways to win versus eight ways to lose.

Luckily, there is a way to minimize this downside, as you will learn ahead in this book.

POINT	PROBABILITY	RETURN	1x PAYS	2x PAYS
4 or 10	2–1	1–2	$10 PAYS $5	$20 PAYS $10
5 or 9	3–2	2–3	$9 PAYS $6	$15 PAYS $10
6 or 8	6–5	5–6	$6 PAYS $5	$12 PAYS $10

FIGURE 11
Free Odds for Don't Pass

COME: In Fig. 12, the *Come* areas are not hard to find. The lower section is where the bet is placed, and the numbered boxes are where that bet will be sent by the dealer, once the destination is established on a subsequent roll.

A *Come* bet is identical to a pass line bet; it's *when* the bet is made that sets it apart. At any point after the come-out, you can drop a chip in the come box, and the next number rolled is the point for that bet. The dealer then moves your bet from the come box to one of the six point number boxes. That number becomes the point for that bet. You can then add a *free odds* bet, which he will set atop your (relocated) come bet, slightly off center to maintain separation between the two bet types.

Players who like lots of action often play new come bets and take odds with every roll of the dice, but not for very long. One little 7 will bring them all down.

There may be times when it is advantageous to play come bets aggressively. When a hot shooter is scorching the table and you've already made enough profit to put some serious money out there, you might do very well. But understand, there may not be a more efficient way to unmask the evil face of Continuum than to play a never-ending string of come bets!

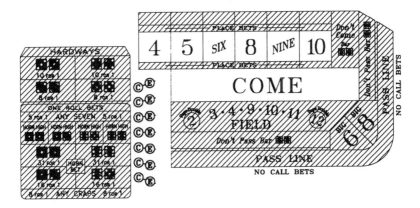

FIGURE 12
The Come Bet Areas

What makes come bets attractive is the multiple come-outs. Remember, a pass line bet has terrific prospects to win during the come-out because the 7 gives the player an instant win. Well, same goes for come bets. Meaning, as your pass line bet loses to a *seven-out,* your come bet might win from the *come-out seven,* thereby defraying the cost of that loss. But don't forget: if you were playing come bets all along, every one that got past the come-out (and is still active) is vulnerable to the seven.

The biggest flaw in the come bet is that (unlike *place bets*) once the bet is up, it's up to stay. You can't remove or reduce it. And there will be times when you'll wish you could.

This description of come bets is intentionally brief, because I don't wish to invest valuable space talking about a type of bet that is adored by compulsive gamblers, and, which has the potential to trigger those inclinations in others.

There are times when come bets *are* recommended, if one takes care not to get carried away. One such time is for a strategy called *Multi-line,* which is described ahead. The only other time is to capitalize on a hot shoot, *provided* that you're financing those bets with money that was recently won.

DON'T COME: *Don't come* is the inverse to *come* just like *don't pass* is to *pass.* The player drops his bet in the don't come box, and after the point *(for that bet)* is established, the dealer puts the bet *behind the line* (the uppermost part of the *point* boxes), at which time odds can be added.

Most bettors who play don't come do so as an expansion of their don't pass bets. They like the idea that (unlike come bets) their bets *win* simultaneously, and *lose* one at a time.

Betting the don't come is a study in precision timing. If the shooter sevens-out against the main point too quickly, it will nail the don't come bet as it is coming out, but too long a roll will shoot down all the bets like ducks in a row. If you pace yourself you might do OK, but one needs a good deal of experience to play this bet successfully.

FIELD: The *Field* is another conspicuous area of the craps layout, and it must look rather tempting to the beginner. Here's a bet that covers seven of the eleven numbers, never pays less than even money, and sometimes pays 2–1.

Obviously, there's a catch, or everyone in the world would play the field. The answer of course is that the four numbers not covered are the most frequently-rolled combinations.

Consider the 7, a non-field number, which by itself can be rolled in as many ways as field numbers 2, 3, 11 & 12 *combined*. What you're doing is comparing seven semi-longshots with the top four favorites, and the latter have the edge.

Field bets are one-roll bets, which means that a win or lose decision will be rendered on the next roll. They carry a house edge of 5.55%, except in some casinos where a 3–1 payoff on the 12 is offered, reducing the vigorish to 2.70%.

Most books say the field is a sucker bet, noting that the craps table offers much better deals—which is true—though there are times when it pays to bet the field. Sometimes, field numbers show up in strings of seven or more. One time, in fact, I made $150 from a three-stage parlay of a $10 field bet.

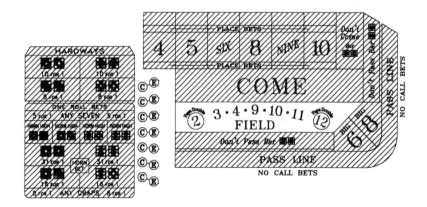

FIGURE   13
The Field

Figure 14 shows the dice combination relationship between field and non-field numbers:

FIELD NO.	COMBINATIONS	WAYS ROLLED	PAYOFF
2	1 + 1	1	2–1
3	1 + 2, 2 + 1	2	1–1
4	1 + 3, 3 + 1, 2 + 2	3	1–1
9	3 + 6, 6 + 3, 4 + 5, 5 + 4	4	1–1
10	4 + 6, 6 + 4, 5 + 5	3	1–1
11	5 + 6, 6 + 5	2	1–1
12	6 + 6	1	2–1

NON-FIELD	COMBINATIONS	WAYS ROLLED
5	1 + 4, 4 + 1, 2 + 3, 3 + 2	4
6	1 + 5, 5 + 1, 2 + 4, 4 + 2, 3 + 3	5
7	1 + 6, 6 + 1, 2 + 5, 5 + 2, 3 + 4, 4 + 3	6
8	2 + 6, 6 + 2, 3 + 5, 5 + 3, 4 + 4	5

FIGURE   14
Dice Combination Comparison

The number of ways field numbers can be rolled comes to eighteen (the sixteen shown plus two to compensate the 2–1 returns on the 2 & 12). But non-fields can be rolled twenty ways, giving the house a 20–18 advantage. But you probably know by now that any team with the 7 on their side is gonna be tough.

PLACE: *Place bets* can be made on any or all of the six point numbers (4, 5, 6, 8, 9 and 10). Each bet stays active until a 7 is rolled (which kills it), or until you decide to call it *off* (render it inactive), or have it physically removed from the layout. The appeal of place bets is threefold:

1) *Each bet can win a multitude of times.*
2) *Each pays better than even money,* and
3) *They can be added or removed throughout the game.*

The figure below shows *where* the dealer positions place bets on the layout. In this illustration, three bettors have *placed the 5,* and there's room for five more bets. The positioning of place bets corresponds to where the players stand around the table. Anyone making place bets should learn the arrangement (while playing) so he can keep an eye on his bets.

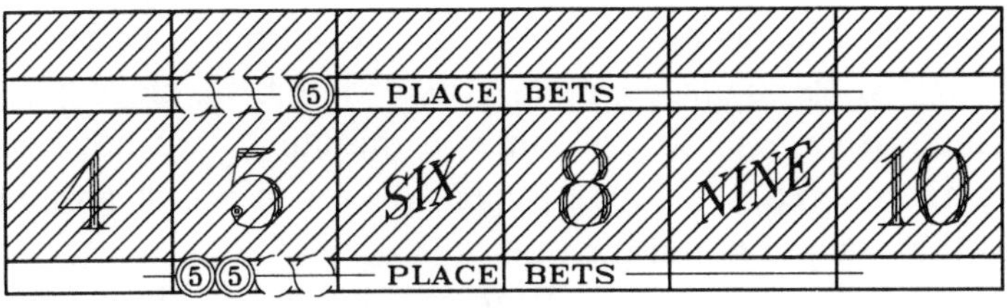

FIGURE 15
The Place Bet Area

NUMBER	WIN PROBABILITY	RETURN	HOUSE EDGE
4 OR 10	1–2	9–5	6.67%
5 OR 9	2–3	7–5	4.00%
6 OR 8	5–6	7–6	1.52%

FIGURE 16
Place Bet Probabilities And Returns

The return for place bets is just a notch below what you would get for your odds bet on a pass line wager. A place bet on the 4 or 10 pays 9–5, which is just below the 2–1 odds bet return. The 7–5 return on the 5 or 9 is just below the 3–2 return for those numbers, and the 7–6 payoff for placing the 6 or 8 is just a tiny bit below the 6–5 free odds return. The 1.52% house edge on a *placed* 6 or 8 is a terrific deal, since these numbers are the most frequently rolled of all numbers except the 7. Most players favor placing the 6 and the 8 over the other numbers.

To a beginner, this may sound fantastic: a bet that pays better than even money, wins indefinitely and can be taken down at any time. . .*where's the downside?*

There are two: first of all, the 7 is seldom very far away from any point in the game. In my experience, placing four or more numbers acts like a magnet for the 7. Even trying to find a window in which you can place six numbers just long enough to catch one or two hits seems like nothing short of impossible most of the time. The second reason is that Continuum does some of its dirtiest work to place bettors. Like come bets, place bets offer a chance to cash in several times a minute if you have several numbers covered. It's great when the seven is not around, but that's the exception, not the rule.

If it's hard resisting the temptation when the rest of the table is cashing in on place bets, just remember that those are the same players that keep the casinos profitable!

Place bets on all numbers except the 6 and 8 should be of an amount that is divisible by five, because the 7–5 return on 5 or 9, and the 9–5 for the 4 or 10 have a 5 as the second digit. (The first number of a bet return represents what you get paid; the second is what you risk.) So, when placing the 4, 5, 9 or 10, any bet amount not divisible by 5 will result in the player getting shortchanged in the course of rounding.

Place bets on the 6 or 8, however, must be divisible by 6, for the 7–6 return requires it. You *can* place the 6 or 8 for $5, but your return will be even money, as the dealer may point out. A 7–6 return means you make $7 profit from a $6 bet, which is a strange bet return; not seen anywhere but at a craps table.

On those rare occasions when you're lucky enough to catch a red-hot table, there's nothing like place bets, pressed up as you win, to help you make money fast. According to a former CEO of the Claridge in Atlantic City, his casino once took a $500,000 hit by a player capitalizing on a hot roll.

But don't be fooled. Place bettors are often the biggest losers of all. Moderation is the key.

BUY BETS: As an alternative to place bets, casinos allow you to *Buy* the number and get paid full odds, minus a 5% commission. For some numbers, this is a good deal.

Now, for the 6 and 8, this option makes no sense because the house edge for placing those numbers is 1.52%, well below the 5% commission. Same for the 5 and 9, with it's 4% vig. But the vig for placing the 4 or 10 is 6.67%. Here, the *buy* option looks pretty good, as long as your bet is $20 or more.

Why $20? Most casinos insist on a $20 minimum for buy bets, because they don't want to bother making change from a $1 chip that would be used to pay the commission. Others simply charge a $1 minimum, in which case the bettor would pay more than 5% through rounding. So, for bets under $20, buy bets are either not allowed, or not profitable to the player.

How do buy bets compare with place bets in dollar amounts? *Placing* the 10 for $25 would return $45, but *buying* the 10 would involve paying $26 ($25+$1 commission) to get a (2–1) $50 return. A net of $49 for $26 certainly beats $45 for $25.

Buy bets aren't marked on the layout, but are positioned by the dealer in the point boxes (like a come bet), with a *buy* button set on top to clarify the wager.

Switching over to different bet types at different intervals may sound confusing, but once you've been around the block a couple times, it'll be second nature to you.

LAY BETS: Several years ago in Atlantic City, I was passing through the craps section at Trump Castle, looking for an opportunity to make the last bet of the day. I stopped at the $25 minimum table, which had only one player, a heavyset dude who had just rolled two consecutive 7s. I watched him roll a third 7, and said to myself, *This table is perfect for a lay bet.* I had my money ready and was expecting him to then roll a point number, but he rolled another 7, his fourth. Then he proceeded to roll two more, and boy, I was nearly salivating in anticipation of the (seemingly) sure bet I was about to make.

On the seventh roll, comes a 10. Damn! Not the number I wanted. Too expensive to lay. But a decision had to be made, so I put $310 on the table and said *"Lay the 9."* On the next roll I won $200 when the shooter sevened out.

Looking back, it would appear that I was not as aggressive as I could've been. Instead of winning one bet, I could have won five, for every 7 he rolled would have represented another win. And, a *Big Red Parlay* (ahead in this book) would have padded my winnings even further.

But I was nonetheless pleased. The day's final wager was successful, and it was time to go eat. There was no way I could have anticipated such a trend from a random walk-up to a table; my bet was practical and sensible. But this story helps me to illustrate a point: that was about as sure a bet as I have ever seen, yet there is *never* a sure bet. That's why I chose the 9 instead of the 10. Less risk to the bankroll.

Lay wagers are bets that can be made at any point during a game, and they pay the true *odds* minus a 5% commission. You can make a lay wager against any (or all) of the six point numbers. This bet wins if a 7 is rolled before the number you have chosen to lay odds against, but after it wins, the dealer will probably take it down immediately. If you want the bet back up, you may have to tell him (or her) so.

Why did I feel the 10 was too expensive to lay, and choose the 9 instead? Just like the *odds* bets, the payoff ratio varies according to the number. I was seeking middle ground between a safe, and lucrative, bet. Please see Figure 17, below:

NUMBER	COST	WIN	PROFIT
4 OR 10	$40 + $1 ($41)	$20	$19
5 OR 9	$30 + $1 ($31)	$20	$19
6 OR 8	$24 + $1 ($25)	$20	$19

FIGURE 17
Lay Bet Cost And Profit

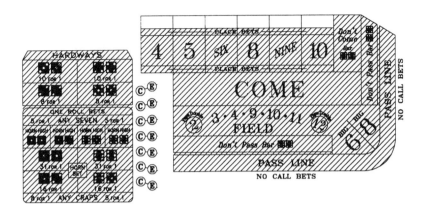

FIGURE 18
The Lay Bet Areas
*(Also referred to as **Behind The Line**)*

To make a lay bet, drop your money on the layout and tell the dealer (for example) *"$31 no nine"* or *"Lay the nine,"* and give him the proper amount (or a multiple thereof), as denoted in Figure 17. He will remove the $1 commission—which you have included—and put the remaining chips *behind the line* (the area shown in Figure 24) for that number. Figure 17 shows the cost of laying the six numbers for a bet large enough to win exactly four units in each case. For every $20 (four units) you attempt to win, the commission is $1. Most casinos don't allow lay wagers at levels below those shown in Figure 17 because of the problem making change from a $1 chip. But if allowed, you would be paying more than you should through rounding, which is not a good idea anyway.

To determine the amount of money needed for bets at other levels, you must know the odds of the desired number, then add the 5% house commission. Calculating the *No Nine* wager I made at Trump Castle was easy: the payoff is 2–3, so you need three units ($300) to win two ($200), then you add $5 for the (5%) commission for every $100 you stand to win.

The value of this bet lies in the fact that you can bet on the side of the seven (and *against* the number of your choice) without having to go through the come-out gauntlet, which is no piece of cake for back line bettors. The only penalty is the 5% commission, which strikes me as a reasonable price to pay for the privilege of getting your man on base.

Laying the 5 or 9 returns 2–3 as stated; laying the 4 or 10 pays 1–2, and the 6 or 8 pays 5–6. As you can see, the 4 or 10 are costly to lay, but lay bets against the 6 or 8 pay close to even money. Quite a difference. I picked on the 9 because it felt safer than laying the 6 or 8, which are statistically the most likely numbers to be rolled *after a seven*. But I didn't want to pay the huge *one-for-two* penalty that accompanies the 10, regardless of the better odds. And there's another reason I didn't want the 10. Back-to-back rolls of the same number frequently occur, and I didn't want to take that chance on my day's last bet.

That being the case, I felt safer with the 9.

BIG 6 & BIG 8: *Big 6* and *Big 8* bets do not appear on layouts in Atlantic City, but you'll find them in Nevada and on most riverboats, in the corners of the layout, between the field and the pass line. These bets are positioned by the player, pay even money, and stay active until they win or lose, however many rolls that may take. If you bet on Big 6, for example, you will win if a 6 is rolled before a 7, unless you pull up your bet, which is permitted. The same, of course, applies for the Big 8.

Why would anyone play these bets (with their 9.09% vigorish) and settle for even money, when they can place the same numbers (for 1.52%) and get a 7 to 6 return?

Well, either those people are too timid to disturb the dealer, too lazy, or else they're profligate morons who don't know better.

But these are just theories of mine.

Most Las Vegas casinos carry Big 6 and 8, but not Bally's. They feel these bets insult the intelligence of their clientele. And that's how you should see it, if you're serious.

PROPOSITION BETS: These are located in the center of the layout (except for some bets which are not marked), and are made by the stickman. So, when making a proposition bet, toss your chips toward him, not the dealer.

As common practice, these bets should not figure prominently in your betting routine, for they've been mathematically constructed to favor the house in a lopsided manner. Nevertheless, there are times when they have their place, for exploiting conspicuous trends or hedging primary wagers.

Please refer to Figure 19 for all proposition bet descriptions in the upcoming pages.

```
                    HARDWAYS
            ┌──────────────┬──────────────┐
            │   10 FOR 1    │   10 FOR 1    │
   (E)(C)   ├──────────────┼──────────────┤  (C)(E)
            │   8 FOR 1     │   8 FOR 1     │
   (E)(C)   ├──────────────┴──────────────┤  (C)(E)
            │        ONE ROLL BETS         │
   (E)(C)   │ 5 FOR 1  ANY SEVEN  5 FOR 1  │  (C)(E)
            │HORN HIGH│HORN HIGH│HORN HIGH│HORN HIGH│
   (E)(C)   │         │         │         │         │  (C)(E)
            ├──────────┴──────────┬────────┘
   (E)(C)   │                      │               │  (C)(E)
            │ 31 FOR 1   HORN      31 FOR 1        │
   (E)(C)   │            BET                        │  (C)(E)
            │                                       │
   (E)(C)   │ 16 FOR 1           16 FOR 1           │  (C)(E)
            │   8 FOR 1   ANY  CRAPS   8 FOR 1      │
            └───────────────────────────────────────┘
```

FIGURE 19
The Proposition Bet Area

HARDWAY: Back on page 35 I referred to a time I held the dice for forty minutes at the Sands in Atlantic City. During that roll, a player at the other end of the table had the *Hard 6* and the *Hard 8* covered with $50 each. At some point I rolled a hard 8, and he was paid $450, and then later he made another $450 on a hard 6. In gaming, those are called big, lucky wins.

Hardways are bets made that *doubles* will show up on the dice (for any of the four *even* point numbers) before a 7, or an *easy* way. A *Hardway 6* (also called a *Hard 6)* is a dice showing of 3 and 3; an *Easy 6* is any other combination adding up to six, such as 4 and 2. For the hard 6 or 8, the payoff is 9 to 1 and the vig is 9.09%. For the hard 4 or 10, the return is 7–1 with an 11.1% edge. Unless the player specifies otherwise, these bets are always working during midgame (after the come-out), and usually *off* during the pass line come-out. Don't be fooled by casinos offering *10 for 1* or *8 for 1.* They equal *9 to 1* and *7 to 1,* respectively.

How do you know when a hardway number will be rolled? If any readers know, please write to me, care of the publisher. I'll pay handsomely for that information if it's reliable!

Most players seem to bet the hardways whenever a shooter is having an extended roll. I think they do so because they are money ahead, and feel lucky. Why not go for it?

Then again, some are prodded into action after hearing the stickman's commercials. He's trained, of course, to promote the bets most advantageous to the house.

Are hardways good bets? For most players, they are not, for they are merely seeking the thrill of catching an occasional longshot, but most of their money gets sucked into that whirling tidepool called the house edge. Others like myself make use of them as hedge bets when playing the back line. In such case, I *do* consider them useful, if played selectively.

For example, a large don't pass bet against the 8 will give you five ways to lose (if an 8 is rolled) and six ways to win (if a 7 is rolled first). The odds are marginally on your side. But if you put a small hedge on the hard 8, you now have *seven* ways to win versus *four* ways to lose. Sounds better to me, though I admit that I often skip the hedge to save money.

How big should you hedge? Just enough to get most of your money back, should your bet go down to a hardway.

Are hardway bets otherwise advisable? Not really, but if you find a way to make them pay, I won't try to stop you.

ANY CRAPS: *Any Craps* is a one-roll bet that covers the three numbers called *craps* during a come-out. It wins if a 2, 3, or 12 is rolled, and pays 7–1.

This bet is most often played as a hedge to protect a pass line bet against an immediate loss from a craps number (rolled during the come-out). You'll still lose your pass line bet, but you will win the *any craps* bet.

Most players prefer playing the pass line bareback, that is, with no hedge. The ones that do use it usually put up $1 for every $10 wagered on the pass line. Others forego the hedge until their first *craps* loss, *then* they start hedging.

Is it a good bet? Most books say no, because of the 11.1% house edge. But it's one of my favorite bets.

When playing pass line, I want to get my man on base. Why risk everything on one roll? When hedging the pass line, there's one thing you know for sure: no way can you lose (big) on the next roll. You'll either win from a natural, or from the hedge, or witness the point establishment. For that brief moment in time, you're covered every which way.

Few things in life will make you feel like a bigger loser than when you keep getting hammered at the come-out of a pass line bet. That's when the odds are *soooo* in your favor, but persnickity trends are always out there.

The best way to play *any craps* is to hold off until you lose to a craps roll. If it feels like it's the start of a major *craps roll* trend, keep playing it for awhile, for protection. If not, it may be best to stop playing it. This reduces the house edge, because you're responding only to the immediate need.

When you've played this game awhile, you will come to realize that extended come-outs (four or more successive craps/naturals) are pretty routine. When that occurs, the other players are riding a monetary roller coaster—losing, winning, losing, winning—while you're turning over money every step of the way.

Everyone has their own theories about *any craps,* but as I see it, that's the way to do it.

HORN BETS: A *Horn* bet is a one-roll combination bet that covers the *any craps* numbers (2, 3 & 12) plus the 11. This bet is accepted only in dollar amounts that are divisible by 4, for each of the four units wagered pays according to the return for that number. Most casinos pay 15–1 for the 3 and 11, and 30–1 for the 2 and 12. The vigorish for the 3 and 11 bets is 11.1%; for the 2 and 12 it is 13.89%.

A wager that covers four longshots might sound good, but the problem is that the return from the number that wins is diluted by the other bets that automatically lose. Two shots at a 30–1 return and two at 15–1 *sounds* good, but all you're really getting is 3–1 for the 3 or 11, or roughly 7–1 for the 2 or 12.

Most players who bet the Horn do so after a Horn number is rolled (expecting a repeat from that group), or as an expanded hedge during the pass line come-out. But the point of a hedge bet is protection. Why finance coverage of an 11, which is a pass line winner anyway?

Unless you're looking for ways to lose your money, there aren't really any good reasons to make this bet.

HORN HIGH: This bet was designed to maximize the efficiency of the *Horn* as a shearing tool for the bleating, blinking, bacchanalian sponge-heads who don't know better than to play it. Oops! I hope I didn't offend somebody there.

Rather than deal with a four-unit bet, the player can call out *"Horn, high eleven,"* for example, and throw out a nickel. This gives an extra unit of coverage on whatever number may be desired. It caters to those who are either too lazy to bother with the change, or else they feel that calling out the bet makes them sound like they know what they're doing.

I admit, it *sounds* impressive.

Check the face of the boxman the next time you hear someone call out a bet like that. He's probably trying to hide the smile on his face, because he knows he just reeled in another fish without having to use any meaningful bait.

WORLD BETS: This bet is something of a puzzle, for it is seldom mentioned in books, and it doesn't appear on the layouts. Only by playing the game and hearing it called out do you acquire an awareness of its existence.

I have a theory on why it isn't shown on the craps layouts: the casinos are too embarrassed to proclaim it a legitimate bet, for it's even worse than the horn. You heard me.

Actually, the world bet *is* a horn bet, plus a fifth unit going to the *any seven.* The idea is to cover everything that's not a point number; meaning all the *craps* and *naturals,* wrapped up together in one sweet, silly little wager.

This is not a smart bet to make. If a 7 is rolled, all it pays is enough to finance replacing the bet. You don't make a dime off the fact that you won. In the meantime, the extra unit dilutes all the other payoffs even further than the horn.

THREE-WAY CRAPS: Imagine, if you will, the horn bet minus the yo (11). There you have it: *three-way craps.* Like the horn, each bet is paid as a separate wager, and the vigorish is as stated for those three numbers of the horn bet. Some players prefer this option over *any craps* as a pass line hedge, because the return is better if a 2 or 12 is rolled, and I suppose they like those little bonuses from time to time. But, the bet also costs more, and has to be made in amounts that are divisible by three.

If you're seeking to hedge the pass line, stick to the flat 7–1 return of *any craps.* It's more versatile.

TWO-WAY CRAPS: If you play enough craps, you'll eventually hear someone call out *"Two-way craps,"* and you might wonder what it is. Actually, it's not a bet in the typical sense. What that bettor is doing is requesting an any craps for himself and another for the dealers, as a toke.

When I'm doing well at the table, I generally call out *two-way craps* enough times to ensure that they win with me once or twice. But that's up to the individual.

C&E BETS: If you refer back to Figure 19 on page 65, you'll see a series of connected circles with the letters *C* & *E* imprinted therein. The *C* & *E* stand for *Craps* and *Eleven,* and the circles are fanning out to (sort of) aim themselves towards the bettors, to help indicate whose bet is whose.

The *C* & *E* bet is exactly what it appears to be: a bet that covers *any craps* (paying 7–1) and the *11* (paying 15–1), if one of the four numbers (2, 3, 11 or 12) comes up on the next roll. It is basically a condensed *horn,* and considered to be a two-unit bet, but the stickman will accept nickel bets to cover the pair. Also, you can bet either one individually.

This wager is usually made by pass line bettors during the come-out, and it's surprising how many players are suckered into playing it, for it is half hedge (against a craps roll) and half bonus (adding to the come-out win if an 11 is rolled). It is presumed that the only reason this bet is played is because the stickman snags a few pigeons after promoting it.

Again, you've got the problem of payoffs diluted by the other bet component, for the two cannot win simultaneously. But if this bet is separated, suddenly it makes sense. There are times when you may want to bet any craps, and there may be times you'll want coverage of the 11. Both can serve as hedges, but for different bets. In a case such as this, the stickman will place your bet in the applicable circle.

As a combination bet, C & E stinks. But as separate bets, the two have legitimate places in this world.

PROPOSITION LONGSHOTS: If you can imagine taking the horn bet, lighting its fuse and exploding it into four separate bets, you'd end up with *Proposition Longshots.* You have *Aces* (the 2), *Boxcars* (the 12), *Ace-Deuce* (the 3), and the *Yo* (the 11). The 2 and 12 each pay 30–1 and the 3 and 11 return 15–1 in most casinos. But take note: some casinos pay only 29–1 and 14–1, respectively. And they describe these bets as 30 *for* 1 and 15 *for* 1, in an effort to disguise their wanton disregard for your attempts at frugality.

Oh dear. Did I offend some casinos? Sorry.

Some who play these bets are looking for a *repeater,* so they bet on the *ace-deuce* (3), using the appearance of the 3 as their betting trigger. Now, I realize I'm disgracing myself when I say this, but it seems to me that the 3 and 11 often come up in pairs, or one after the other. And I suspect that one could do well going after these longshots. But you'll never understand these intuitions until you've played the game.

Like the horn bet, which is the accumulation of all these options, these are one-roll bets made through the stickman, and can be bet individually or in groups. I've played all of them on different occasions (except for the *aces*). You may decide that some of them are usable for you as well. But be advised, the house edge for all of these bets is in two digits.

PS: If you hear someone call out *high/low,* this is a bet on the 2 & 12. Similarly, *ace-deuce/yo* equals 3 & 11. And *midnight* is sometimes used to request a bet on the 12, in lieu of the word *boxcars.*

HOP BETS: At this writing, as far as I know, *Hop* bets are not available in Atlantic City or the riverboats, but they *are* offered in Las Vegas. But then, what isn't offered in Vegas? They'll give you odds on how many times your weiner dog takes a dump, if you provide enough data.

A Hop is a one-roll wager on a specific dice combination that can occur in two ways, such as 5 and 4 (equaling a 9). A *Hop Hardway* is also a one-roller, but on a number that can be rolled only one way, such as 5 and 5.

Payoffs for these bets can vary from 14–1 to 15–1 for the Hops and 29–1 to 30–1 for the Hop Hardways. The vigs for these wagers range from 11.1% to 16.67%, no bargain.

One of the first times I heard this bet called out, it was the player to my right requesting *"4 and 4 on the hop"* as he tossed a nickel to the stickman. The next roll was a 4 and 4, and the man didn't even blink. Until I figure out how he did that, I think you would be better off avoiding this bet.

ANY SEVEN:

This is the worst bet on the table, bar none.

    —John Patrick, *John Patrick's Craps*

Avoid this bet at all costs.

    —Edwin Silberstang, *Guide to Casino Gambling*

An inadvisable, sucker proposition.

    —Tom Ainslie, *How to Gamble in a Casino*

Of all the bets at craps, this is the ultimate, the very worst.

    —Arthur S. Reber, *The New Gambler's Bible*

  If you read the above, it certainly appears that a compelling verdict has been reached on the *any seven*. Poor little any seven, the bet that nobody likes.

  What's wrong with this bet? Isn't seven the number that destroys pass line bets, place bets, and field bets? Wouldn't it make sense to align oneself with the Great Destroyer?

  Not when the bet pays only 4–1 for taking a 5–1 chance. That's 16.67% you're fighting, the toughest edge at the table. This bet is so bad, you shouldn't even say its name out loud—during midgame—at the table where you make it.

  Any Seven is a one-roll proposition bet that pays 4–1, but you are advised to ask for it by the name *Big Red,* except during the come-out. Why? Well, you want to keep living, don't you? Then don't infuriate all the pass line bettors who dread hearing anything that sounds remotely like that unmentionable word 'seven' between come-outs. Even if someone asks you the time at 7:17 pm, just hide your watch and say you don't know!

  Now that you know what a rotten bet the *any seven* is, this is a good time to inform you that everything you know is wrong. Because I'm going to try to vindicate the any seven.

To help you understand why my opinion of any seven differs so sharply from that of the experts, let us first take a look at why they don't like it:

Is it the 16.67% house edge? That's it. To them, 16-plus tells the whole story. To advocate the any seven is to reveal one's stupidity. Turn the page and close the book.

Now take a look at the other side. It is an indisputable fact that the most likely number to be rolled consecutively is the 7. But what about three, four, five in a row? Happens all the time. My records show that if you play craps for six hours, there's a good chance you'll run into *six* triple sevens, and one of those is likely to go four-in-a-row.

So how does one capitalize on this? What you'll be looking for is a run of three sevens. The first one is your betting trigger. Then you play big red for a nickel. If that wins, press it to $20. This is not a full parlay, but this way, you'll get your basic bet back if you win the first stage but lose the second.

If you win both stages, you collect $100 profit, and take the bet down. Not a bad score from a $5 bet.

To illustrate, let me tell you about one that I missed, and one I hit, the same day. I was at one of the riverboats in my area, and the shooter's first roll was a 7. Then came three more before he established his point. I tried to kick myself for missing the bet, but my foot wouldn't reach. After a while, I left the table. At the next table, a shooter came out on a 7 again. This time I was ready, and sure enough, he rolled three more, like before. So what looked like a missed opportunity turned out to be the signal that the multiple-seven trend was active in that casino.

No one can explain this, but it happens.

While I realize that the other gaming authors consider me a fool for advocating this bet, there are times when a casino-wide trend is so obvious, that it makes sense to venture a small wager whenever a shooter commences his roll with a 7.

No question, you'll lose a lot of these trials. But the times you win will make up a lot of ground.

Think about it, next time you see a string of 7s.

SUMMARY OF
PROPOSITION BETS

Most knowledgeable people agree that *proposition bets* are bad bets, for they're designed—through mathematical advantage —to favor the house more than the mainstay bets. But it's not as simple as all that.

To a pro, nearly every bet at the craps table is like a surgical instrument. Each has its own specific function, and collectively, they widen one's range of alternatives. Some of these options are expensive, so they must be used discriminately. But to proclaim them all to be monsters based on numerical figures is not, in my opinion, good advice.

Proposition bets enable a player to capitalize upon trends that occur randomly yet routinely in any casino. They are the tools that help one maximize his efficiency. I have seen tables where every shooter rolls at least one 7 at the very beginning of his come-out. That's a catchable trend. Are you going to ignore a predictable wagering opportunity that could enable you to bet with pinpoint precision and reap continuous 4–1 returns because you fear the 16.67% house edge?

The exploitation of trends in gaming is what gambling is all about. To do the job right, you need access to every device at your disposal. Proposition bets, costly though they may be, can work to your advantage.

Casinos are helpless against the wild swings of the dice that occur every day. This is where your advantage lies. Make the most of it, 'cause it's a sink or swim world.

SUMMARY OF CRAPS BETS

Now that you know all the betting options for craps, don't you wish you understood the game?

No tutorial can substitute for one hour of the real thing, and this book is no exception. But if you follow the teachings herein, you can't go too far astray.

Your training period will entail practice games to simulate —and casino visits to observe—live games. And for those who really take it seriously, it wouldn't hurt to pick up some other books on the subject. The more you study the subject, the better you'll understand the games. The best source source for gaming titles (that I am aware of) is the *Gambler's Book Shop* in Las Vegas, at 1-800-522-1777.

This chapter is intended primarily to demonstrate how the game is played and the available options. Some of these options are better than others, but most of them have their place, at some point or another. To do the job right, you need access to all the tricks. And that includes proposition bets. As this author sees it, the bigger your portfolio of betting options, the more effectively you'll be able to tame the trends.

When you bet selectively, you won't feel the house edge, for your bets are triggered only when a specific trend has been identified. This helps you weed out the would-be losses: table decisions that *would have represented* the house edge.

Most players are clueless to the wagering opportunities that are constantly presenting themselves at the tables. You will learn how to capitalize on the trends that breed these opportunities, for that is the specialty of this book.

6

THE MECHANICS
OF GAMING

Keep rowing.

—Mark Powell

Now we must move from the abstract to the precise. What exactly are the moves you'll be making as you forage for income in a casino?

THE BUY-IN

Before you can play craps or any other casino table game, you must first make a buy-in, the conversion of cash into gaming tokens. This was covered briefly in the previous section, but here you will find the details.

Your first consideration is to find a table with space to play, and with a table minimum compatible with your resources.

At a craps table, there is a small placard on one or both of the inside walls of the table, in front of where the dealers stand. This is where the minimum and maximum bets are noted. The minimum is usually on the top line, with oversize lettering, for obvious reasons: this is the most important information, and not all of us have eagle eyes.

For those with really poor vision, there is a way to get a clue about the table minimum. The color of the placard will often be a good tipoff. A red sign will almost always indicate a $5 minimum table, and green is standard for a $25 table. Sign colors for the $10 and $15 tables are usually blue and yellow, but not necessarily in that order. I have seen the same casino use yellow for a $10 table one month, and blue the next. But red and green are pretty standard.

Once you think you've found the table of your dreams, you move up close to the rail and try to get a feel for what's going on. You don't want to be making the transaction as the dice are in the air. Having made that observation, you drop the money on the layout in front of one of the dealers, and say *"Change only."* Whatever you do, don't try to hand him the money. Dealers are not allowed to accept money that way. This is something that all casinos insist on, to help ensure that somebody isn't getting some kind of payoff. Also, the words "Change only" make it clear that you're not trying to make a cash bet on the betting option that is closest to where the money landed.

As he picks up your money, the dealer will usually repeat the words *"Change only"* to the boxman as he hands over the cash to be verified, or counted, if necessary. Then, at the next pause in the game, he'll grab the appropriate amount of chips and place them on the layout in front of you.

If you seek a certain breakdown in the chip denominations, tell the dealer as you drop the money. For example, if you buy in for $500, you might want to specify *"Ninety in reds, ten whites, and the rest in greens, please."* If you don't specify, the dealer might ask if you have a preference, but at a $5 table, most dealers go ahead and give you the standard setup: $100 in red chips for the first hundred, and the rest in greens for buy-ins up to $500. For larger buy-ins, they usually ask your preference.

Then you put the chips in your section of the rail, and you're ready to put down some bets.

When it's time to cash out, wait for a pause in the game, put your chips on the layout, and say, *"Color."*

THE BANKROLL

Before making your buy-in, you're going to have to figure out where to get the money to do so. That money will originate from your *bankroll,* a fund you create to be used exclusively for gaming endeavors.

The size of your bankroll depends on how much money you're willing or able to set up for this purpose. If your average buy-in is $100, for example, it is generally recommended that you back it up with a cash reserve that is twenty times that amount, which would work out to $2000.

Does this sound high to you? Seems a little over the top to me, but the idea is to have the inner knowledge, as you play, that you've got a substantial reserve to back you up if you hit a wall with your strategy. See, you don't want to be caught playing with "scared money," that is, money you're afraid to lose because it's all you've got left in the gaming fund that you established. That will almost certainly cause you to change your tactics when things go poorly, and this usually compounds the damage.

My recommendation is not to exceed 1/10 of your bankroll for any buy-in, but be prepared for a possible loss of your stake. It's not the end of the world, is it?

One last thing you should keep in mind: your bankroll is your toolkit. When it's gone, you're dead in the water. You're just a rotting corpse bobbing on the ebb tide. And the fact on the face of it is: nobody's going to lend you a dime once they know you have a tendency to gamble.

They do that to 'protect you from yourself.'

THE SESSION

Now that you've got a bankroll, your *session* can begin. This is the gaming activity in which you participate, in between the time you buy in and cash out. Ideally, your bankroll should be large enough to finance a number of sessions, each of which represents a financial tug-of-war between you and the casino. Your goal is to win the majority of these battles.

Why is your bankroll subdivided into sessions? The idea is to limit your losses in the event you get caught up in a losing jag. Anything can happen in the short run. You need to take steps to contain the potential damage so you don't blow your wad in one horrible and deeply regrettable moment.

How much money should you invest in a session? Depends on your betting level, how much time you want to invest and any other particulars that may affect your decision. Many recreational players buy in for $100 and play until it's all gone.

You're gonna want to avoid that little trap.

How long does a session last? As long as you decide, or until you can no longer play because of some mega-event like an earthquake or tornado. Of course, Armageddon, or an invasion by evil Martians could also impact the duration of your session. Most of the time, it's your call. You might want to play for an hour or more, or just place a single bet.

Then again, after taking a minute to study the table pattern, you might decide that this table is bad news, in terms of whatever you were looking for. That's okay. You're not required to make a single bet. Just pick up your chips and leave.

THE SERIES

And now we come to the *series.* There's no end to all the stuff you have to learn, is there?

A series, in simple terms, is a betting cycle or progression. It consists of either a single bet or a group of bets, whose number is predetermined by the player.

Some gaming authors say that a series ends only after a win occurs. I disagree. To me, a series ends when:

1) The last bet of a cycle is reached,
2) A convenient stopping point is reached, or
3) A win occurs.

You might decide to craft your own definition of a series, depending on your style of play. But the basic concept is simply a group of bets that are (in some way) connected.

THE PARLAY

On a related subject we come to the *parlay,* although this is more of an *offensive,* rather than *defensive,* tool.

A *parlay* is the technique of adding the proceeds of a successful bet to the very next bet, forming a new, larger wager. This can be applied in one or several stages.

The parlay is one of the neatest tricks ever devised for the player, for it allows one to maximize his gains. Ahead, you will learn more about how it can be applied.

HEDGE BETS

Earlier in the book, there were some references to *hedge bets*. You didn't think I was gonna let you go out there without some kind of explanation, did you?

Hedge bets are similar to auto insurance. In the event of a catastrophic failure, you have some protection. You're entitled to immediate compensation.

Example: You're playing line bets, and your table is putting out a lot of *craps* rolls during the come-out. In that case, I put a little hedge on my bets: *any craps* for pass line and come bets, and *yo* (11) when playing the don't pass or don't come. It helps me keep my temperment in check.

I usually put $1 on the any craps for $10 pass line bets, $2 for the $15 to $20 level, and $3 for $25 bets. On the don't side, I play $1 yo for every $15 to $20 wagered. That leaves the big red uncovered, but that hedge is too expensive for me.

Hedge bets are most useful when a large bet is on the line. That way, your most valuable bets are protected.

Imagine, for example, that you're playing don't pass with $100 chips, and you get burned by three straight 11s. If you play long enough, you'll run into table trends like that. How are you gonna feel after losing $300, when a $5 hedge on the yo would have returned four-fifths of what you lost?

My recommendation is to play these hedges only as noted above, with the occasional exception of hedging your very first bet at the table. Losing that first bet because you didn't hedge is a tough way to start a session!

CHARTING A TABLE

If you spend enough time in casinos, you may come across the term "charting a table." This is not as complicated as it might sound. All this means is that you're taking some time, before you send your soldiers (dollars) out there, to see what kind of results the table is putting out.

To some people, I realize, this will sound stupid. All table results are independent events, right? What's the point of looking things over if the future at any table is an unknown?

Well, experience has taught me that you want to have some kind of idea of the battlefield conditions before jumping out into the fray. At some tables you'll see nothing but seven-outs every third or fourth roll. At others, you'll see lots of numbers being rolled between the line bet decisions. Those trends could change in the blink of an eye, but why fight what looks like an obvious trend, that is contrary to your chosen strategy? Those trends can hang on for what seems like forever. Don't waste your time and money on them. Seek out greener pastures.

Some players I know cling to the belief that all tables are equal, and so there is no point in moving. Ever. I see them get hammered for thousands, playing the front line at tables that are colder than an igloo on Jupiter. Then they buy in for another three thousand, and maybe they'll finally catch a piece of something. But they're doing it the hard way.

Trends can be powerful. It's just not smart to disregard the fact that you're riding the bummer express. Get out of there. Find another table. You came to win, didn't you?

THE COMFORT ZONE

If your bets aren't large enough to hurt you, it won't do you any good to win.

—Bill Lear

Imagine that you were playing a casino table game at the $5 level, and you had won $60 in thirty minutes. You had made a prior decision to keep your bets at the nickel level until obtaining some assurance that your (experimental) strategy was sound. As you were accumulating this information, you projected mentally to the figure you would have won had you played with the black ($100) chips instead of the reds ($5 chips). Sounds like a simple mathematical conversion, doesn't it?

Indeed it is, if you're just playing with figures in your head. But when you're using the black chips for real, your hands are gonna shake, your palms are gonna sweat, and you're gonna feel like a fat pigeon on the hot pavement.

Now you've done it. You're all alone, frightened, and in the dark. And it's all because you strayed too far from the warmth and safety of your own personal *Comfort Zone*.

At the nickel level, you were doing okay once you got past the first four bets, which were losses. Being down twenty bucks is no big deal. But if those bets were made with blacks instead of reds, you'd be out $400, and buddy, you'd feel *that* loss. Would you have done the same thing at that point, as you did with the red chips? Sorry to say, the greater chance is that you wouldn't. Consequently, that $1200 figure derived from your conversion would be a primrose fantasy.

This is what happens when you play outside that venerable perimeter known as the *Comfort Zone.* Reaching your ideal betting level is a mentality that must be worked toward in stages. You're not going to make it in a single leap. Actually, you might get there, but you won't last.

While living in Las Vegas some years ago, I decided to go to the Frontier every night after work during a two-week period, in an attempt to pick up an extra $50 to $100 per night, playing craps. It worked great: at the end of twelve consecutive winning days, my bankroll had grown from an initial stake of $100, to over $1100. That was all the proof I needed. I was on my way. It was time to go for larger gains!

Naturally, that's when the losses came. I tried to bet my way out of the crisis with even larger bets, using timing as an excuse to legitimize my compulsion. But the first night of play at the higher levels, I blew the entire bankroll I had worked so hard for two weeks to acquire, plus the original stake. Then, after licking my wounds, I pulled myself off the pavement and tried again, managing to build up *another* $1000 over the next two weeks. . .only to lose every last dollar *again* on the night I chose to go for larger gains!

You know, you tell yourself that it just can't happen again. It just can't. To believe otherwise is to surrender to superstition. But what do you do when it *does* happen? How in God's name can you explain that to anyone?

How can you explain it to yourself?

Take note, readers. This is the kind of runaround you get when you spend time in casinos.

My mistake was trying to move up too soon. If I'd waited until I had built up $3000 instead of $1000, it might've worked. It seems like an absurd extension of what should be necessary, but that's how it is. Moving up the ranks of betting levels is an unerringly difficult proposition.

I thought my goals were reasonable, but it wasn't enough. Moral is: without a seemingly preposterous amount of patience and discipline, you're gonna get whipped.

THE MAGIC DOWNSIDE NUMBER

Just a little postscript to conclude this section. I hope you don't mind that this pertains to roulette.

Very early in my casino gaming career, I undertook the task of gathering information about roulette trends. Part of my research was directed toward finding the magic number for the downside of a bet. Meaning, what was the maximum number of spins an even money bet, for example, could possibly go without appearing? Tee hee. I sought a number that could be relied upon absolutely, so that if a table ever reached that figure, I'd be assured a winner on the next bet. Hah hah hah. That was before I understood trends. I guess I was thinking that eventually, the law of averages would begin *dictating to the table.*

When I played at a table in Vegas where red did not show for eighteen spins, I knew it was a lost cause. By the way, black didn't win all of those; two zeroes got in there.

During that period and beyond, I witnessed some strange things. A table at the Sands casino, for example, where 0 or 00 didn't show for over 150 spins, next to one where they came up 7 out of 35. You can't fight trends like that.

Chances are, the day you pick to bludgeon your way to a win is the day a table trend will make it to the evening news, and you happened to have backed the wrong side. The very thought is the gambler's worst nightmare.

Expect them every couple weeks or so.

In short, the *magic downside number* is a godforsaken place that doesn't even exist!

PART II

PROFESSIONAL TECHNIQUES

7

YOUR DEFENSIVE ARSENAL

Back on page 7, it was noted that before you can learn to win, you must learn how to *not lose*. What that says, is that even the most dynamic offense in the world doesn't mean much if it's not supported with an outstanding defense.

SESSION LOSS LIMITS

Of all the weapons in your defensive arsenal, none are more requisite to your success than strict adherence to your *loss limits,* as they pertain to each session, and each day.

Loss limits are your most cherished allies. They are there to protect you from yourself and from the evil you would do in their absence. They are what separate you from the losers, charlatans and fools. They confer the protection you absolutely need to do the job you have to do.

Now if you only knew what I'm talking about.

The concept of *session loss limits* is pretty simple. Before buying in at any table, you must visualize a figure in your head that represents the maximum damage you're willing to sustain in the event that things don't go well. When swimming in a pool of sharks, you have to acknowledge the possibility that one of them might manage to remove a pound of your flesh. The sharks, mind you, are trained to strip away wealth from all those who enter the gates, and they're good at what they do.

Loss limits are your most important line of defense. Until you learn this, gaming will be one long struggle in the dark.

Those who succeed at casino gambling and those who write how-to books about it, all have their own theories about loss limits. It's not a black-and-white matter. Many authors advocate setting your loss limits at a figure representing *half* your buy-in. That means, you're going to stop playing when half your chips are gone; the remaining half are never to be used. According to them, it is psychologically bad to leave the table with empty pockets, or to bet down to your last chip.

The underlying principle of that argument makes sense to me, but what's important is seeking out a way to mitigate the downside, and settling into something that works. Whatever your feelings are, it is essential that you establish a mechanism to keep you from chasing your losses.

At craps, I allow myself the option of depleting my buy-in, and making a secondary buy-in that amounts to half the original figure, because it's a volatile game from which I can swing back. But if things don't turn around pretty quick, I'm out of there. My recommendation is that you seek a method that works for you, and then, before buying in, make a promise to yourself and stick to it, every time.

What's really important is this: never, ever let yourself get into the habit of pulling money out of your pocket when you're losing, like you're feeding a vending machine. That is what those esteemed authors are warning about, and they have a good point. The exception I make (noted above) is *planned,* and enacted only when the table shows late-inning potential.

DAILY LOSS LIMITS

Just as important as the session loss limits (which have just been discussed) are *daily loss limits*.

Before heading on down to the casino, you should establish a predetermined figure that represents the absolute *max* you're willing to lose that day—in your quest for disposable income. If you don't do this, there is the chance that one day, you'll find yourself draining every bank account you have, all because you had a bad day and ended up in a panic-stricken frenzy to *quickly!* bail yourself out of the mess you created. Believe me, you have the capacity to do this.

Some players find it prudent to set up bankroll safeguards, so that only so much money can be accessed from all sources in a given period of time. I recommend that you don't rule out the possibility that you might have to do the same. This subject is covered ahead in *Bankroll Safeguards*.

Generally speaking, loss limits (of any kind) represent the contract you negotiate with yourself in advance. Like the LAPD, they are there to Protect and Serve. Or is it to Serve and Protect? (I can never remember the correct order of those words.)

Never underestimate their importance. Everybody has his preferences in managing his pursuits, but without loss limits, you're gonna need a slick answer to the question:

What do you want on your tombstone?

WIN GOALS

Win goals are your second most important lines of defense. Here's the basic concept: whenever you get ahead at the tables, you need to take steps to ensure that you leave the table a winner. The worst mistake you can make is to press your luck and give all your winnings back to the house.

And then some.

Leaving the table a winner is achieved by locking up your gains as you go, then going for more in stages.

Before the buy-in, along with setting the amount you will allow yourself to lose before retreating, you must also set a figure that you feel you can *realistically* win. The former is your *loss limit;* the latter, your *win goal.*

In doing so, you're able to visualize the full spectrum of what might occur. That's what it takes to win.

SETTLE FOR 90

One thing that has been invaluable in helping me leave the casino a winner is a little trick I call *Settle for 90.*

Necessity was the mother of this invention, for at some point I got tired of repeatedly being 90% to my win goal, then losing everything I had won while trying to get that last 10%. That was before I was tuned into locking up a profit, but it was amazing how many times it happened.

The idea is: don't obsess over an arbitrary figure when you are so close. If you reach a good stopping point, take what the table gave you and be thankful it wasn't a loss. You did good. You gambled and won. Don't press it.

Many are the times I have reached some kind of impasse, and I ask myself whether I should continue playing, or get the heck out of there. Most of those times, if I stay, I end up with deep regrets about doing so.

And I wish I could get back to the place where the question was still being contemplated.

Settle for 90 also serves as a secondary line of defense, in the event of a catastrophic failure of your loss limits. When you have logged some real time at the tables, I'm sure you'll come to make use of this rule as an alternate safety net.

The whole purpose behind manuals like this is to help you avoid all the costly errors that were dearly paid for by those who went before you into the dragon's lair.

All I can do is point the way. The rest is up to you.

THE REALITY CHECK

It is unwise to be too sure of one's wisdom. It is healthy to be reminded that the strongest might weaken and the wisest might err.

—Mohandas Gandhi

Somewhere on the horizon, beyond the principles of loss limits and win goals, there is an overriding principle that covers both, which I call the *reality check*.

The reality check is a promise to yourself to keep your gaming activity strictly monitored. You must question the wisdom of the choices you're making every single minute: Are you accomplishing what you set out to do? Have you adhered to the procedure? Are you in complete and absolute control? You must watch yourself like a hawk, because the minute you let go is the cast-in-stone minute the demons from hell will emerge up from the manholes and seize control.

You need to constantly ask yourself these questions: Am I winning at this table? Is this table helping me or hurting me? If you are losing, you ask: Is it a loss I understand? Or is the table churning out some bizarre trend that's keeping me off balance, or filling me with a seething, quiet rage?

They can do that, you know.

Once a minute is a hard figure. A serious figure. But that's how often you need to step outside yourself and take a look at that idiot who's risking *your money*. What is he doing? Is he on top of things? It's imperative that you challenge every bet he makes and every decision he contemplates.

So what is the procedure for watching oneself?

The thought came to me while playing minibaccarat years ago at the Claridge in Atlantic City. At some point I noticed that I had an audience. A woman in her twenties was standing next to me, and when I glanced up she asked me some questions about the game. She said it looked like fun.

She wanted to play, but the table was full, so I offered to add her chips to my bets, slightly off center.

She had only two or three Reds in her hand when we started, but after thirty minutes she had roughly fifteen. About then, it struck me as a good time to cash out, and I invited her to check out some other casinos with me. That's when she said her bus would be leaving soon. She was just killing time.

Things might have turned out better for me, but that little encounter helped me see the value of an objective, detached stance while at the tables. If you think about it in terms of helping a pretty girl make money, it's easier to acquire the objectivity you need to make good things happen. I realized then that it was easier for me to help *her* than to help myself. With my guidance, she quintupled her "buy-in" in less time than it took for me to double mine.

Setting up your own reality check means reminding yourself before walking up to the tables that you're going to take a time out, every minute, to evaluate how you're doing. Think about what's at stake: a good day at the tables, or not.

SUMMARY ON DEFENSE

Anything that can go wrong will go wrong, and at the worst possible moment.
——Murphy's Law

Gaming is a tricky business. The tables don't think or react to anything we do, and yet legions of men and women are foiled, time after time, generation after generation, by these lifeless, inert objects.

Are we being outwitted by those who have no wits?

So it would seem. But what really happens is we let our guard down. We are unprepared for the unexpected, for it doesn't seem possible for passivity to be so shrewd.

Even after spending a lifetime on the player side of the tables, any veteran of the games knows that he'll never have seen it all. Around every corner in time lurks a new surprise, waiting to shock and amaze us, every one.

Your best defense is to remain humble. To acknowledge that the element of surprise is on the side of the other guy. Expect the worst result at the worst possible moment. If you continue to think in those terms, there is hope.

Have a plan and follow through on it. Don't let yourself be influenced by all the aberrations swimming about, looking for fresh meat. Stay in control.

Most important: watch yourself. Be ready for the beginning of your own self-destruction at any moment, and get out of there before the knife cuts too deep.

Be prepared for the challenge of a lifetime, each and every day you spend time in a casino.

8

SYSTEMS IN GAMING

Many gaming books contain at least a few *systems,* which are close-ended strategies designed to afford the player a superior chance to win over random wagering. Some are simple and some are rather elaborate; some work only half the time and some hardly ever fail. But the latter can be dangerous, because when you lose, you lose BIG.

The unpredictable nature of trends pretty much guarantees that no system is infallible. With enough discipline, however, one might be able to eke out a living by using this system or that. But you'll be fighting tremendous odds, and your life will be as cold and hard as arctic stone.

This book doesn't advocate using systems, though some advanced players may be able to make them work when combined with other procedures. Still, the focus of this book is on *techniques* that will give you excellent chances at the tables. You will be taught to make decisions like a seasoned player, and you'll see the world much as they do. But you'll have to learn to take your losses in stride and, most of all, accept the fact that some days you just can't win.

Nevertheless, this book would not be complete if it didn't let you know what systems are out there, along with a summary of their weaknesses and strengths.

EVEN MONEY SYSTEMS

Most system players prefer even money wagers, for they are found at all major table games, and offer a frequent win rate. They are the most basic wagers found in gaming, and are commonly the backbone of a professional's repertoire. Knowing about the systems designed for these bets should enhance your general understanding of the available options.

MARTINGALE: As systems go, this one exists in a class by itself, for it's the brainchild of easily a billion gamblers. I'm ashamed to admit that I invented it, *after* it was invented by the billion I just spoke of. When I say *invented,* I mean that it was an original idea, but as ideas go, this one is a real dog. I pity the fool who donated his name to this system.

The Martingale was designed for even money wagers, and the concept is disarmingly simple: when you lose, you double the size of your bet. If you keep losing, keep doubling. When you do win, the betting cycle is consummated and you regress to the bet amount you started with.

Neat idea, huh? As long as you don't lose more than, say, seven bets in a row, you'll never lose a series. Now, I can imagine how good this might sound to someone who has never played live bets in a casino, but there's a magnificent flaw here. Any seasoned player knows that losing streaks of nine or ten consecutive even money bets are not uncommon. So, for the sake of argument, let's project the amount you'd need to cover a series that produces a win on the eleventh bet.

Your first bet is $5; when it loses, go to $10. Then go to: 20–40–80–160–320–640–1280–2560, and 5120. Financing those bets costs over $10,000 just to scratch out a $5 profit at the end. But the problem is getting a waiver against the table maximum in the midst of all that, and that's not real likely.

These days, many casinos offer wide ranges between the table minimums and maximums; even the $5 (minimum) tables may have a two or three thousand dollar maximum. But some other places aren't so liberal. In places like those, a Martingale progression that commences with a $5 wager might reach the table maximum somewhere around the seventh step. What I'm saying is: the eleven–stage series I projected may not be possible, even if you were foolish enough to attempt it. That's what we in the business call a supercalifragilistic flaw.

Granted, you could set up an arbitrary ceiling of six wagers (which would cost $315 for a complete cycle), and, you might be able to win hundreds of bets before losing a series. But you're just postponing the inevitable. The day will come when you can't win five bets without suffering a full series loss, and then it happens twice more before you quit for the day. That's when you start seeing the truth about cats and dogs.

Through the years, I've performed thousands of numerical trials. Want to know what I've found? On the average, no matter how many stages you use, you'll encounter a full series loss at roughly the same rate it takes to earn enough units to pay for it. And when you figure in the house edge, the two sets of figures correspond almost exactly. Isn't that a hoot?

MINI-MARTINGALE: The mini version is much less destructive than its cousin, because it is limited to three stages. At the $5 level, the series is 5–10–20. If you don't win at the third stage, write off the series and start over.

A full series costs $35, which is a massive improvement over the thousands a Martingale *could* cost, but there are two problems: You have only three chances to win, and, it will take seven wins to compensate one series loss.

At a choppy table, a MiniMartingale can keep you winning indefinitely. But when the table patterns change, you're gonna get a load of buckshot in your butt.

Some quasi-professionals specialize in the MiniM and have days when they do just fine. But if you're seeking long-range success, this ain't the ticket.

All the same, you could do worse. I use it periodically. Playing the MiniM is a bit like speeding through a yellow light. If you don't do it too much, you may be able to dodge the man for some time. But when you get nabbed, lay off.

ANTI-MARTINGALE: Finally, we come to the last of the Martingales. Once these are out of the way, we can move on to something more meaningful.

The AntiMartingale is the mirror image of the Martingale. You double your bet only when you *win,* not when you lose. Then at some arbitrary point you take a profit, and begin again. It's essentially a multiple-stage parlay.

This system was conceived with the purpose of enabling one to get rich from a very small bet. If played successfully for seven consecutive bets, a $5 bet will earn $635 profit. But how could one anticipate a trend like that? If any readers know and write a book about it, every casino on planet earth will go under. I don't think I'm going to see that in *my* lifetime.

Imagine, for a moment, that you just won six straight bets. Would you have the guts to let it all ride? And if you did and lost, how would you feel? It would feel great before the last decision, when all the other players are cheering you on. But when that seventh bet goes down, don't count on their support. Your fifteen minutes of fame has come and gone. Now, you're just another schmuck who made a foolish bet.

The world is full of people who can do that.

Biggest problem is, when do you take a profit? If you're a bad guesser, you may never win a series.

Keep looking.

THE 31 SYSTEM: Like the Martingale, this one is a progression; that is, a strategy that calls for increasing the bet until a win occurs. With the *31,* a series loss is not as devastating, but you'll feel that loss when it comes.

The 31 System gives you nine chances to win, but you need back-to-back wins at the conclusion of each series. It consists of (up to) nine bets that occur on four levels:

```
LEVEL 1:   1    1    1
LEVEL 2:        2    2
LEVEL 3:        4    4
LEVEL 4:        8    8
```

FIGURE 20
The 31 System Tiers

Playing the 31 System, you start out with a single-unit bet. If that loses, the next bet is also one unit. If once again you lose, you make one more bet at the one-unit level. Should you endure another loss, you move up to level 2 and bet two units. Until you win, keep following the diagram above.

The 31 System is so named because 31 units are required to complete a betting series. At the $5 level, that works out to $155; at the quarter level it's $775. When you finally win (presuming the cycle hasn't been exhausted), you parlay the winning bet. If that bet succeeds, you'll show a profit for that series, regardless of where along the chain the wins occurred.

It sounds ingenious, for you can lose eight consecutive bets and still end up in the black. The trick is, you've got to end up with back-to-back wins.

This system is clever in its conception, but there's one thing about it that bothers me: it doesn't work. When I look over my old scorecards, it's all too clear that this system would have done more harm than good. And THAT is where I draw the line. I'm not looking for ways to bury myself.

For anyone who is not completely clear on how this system works, here are a few examples: Let's say that one unit is $5, and you lose the first bet. The next bet is also $5, and you win. At that point you parlay your bet and win $10. You now have $20, which cost $10 to generate. Your profit is $10.

Now let's look at where you would be if you lost the first five bets, then got your back-to-back wins. From level 1, you'd be out $15 ($5 x 3). Level 2, another $20 ($10 x 2). At the first stage of level 3, your four-unit bet wins. You parlay to eight for the follow-up and win again. You now have $80, and it cost you $55 to do it. Your profit is $25.

If you had come through with the consecutive wins at the second stage of level 3, it would have cost you another four-unit bet ($20), so your profit would be reduced by that amount, leaving you with only a $5 gain. Obviously, you're better off when the first win (of two) occurs at the first—rather than the second—stage of whatever level you're on.

According to Robert Eisenstadt, who applied the 31 System to pass and don't pass bets in a book called *Systems That Win,* one can expect to lose a complete betting series 10.8% of the time. But he admits that his objective is *"to snatch a few victories while the gods of chance are napping."*

Doesn't sound especially solid to me.

D'ALEMBERT: This is also called the *Pyramid.* The idea is to increase the bet by one unit after each loss and reduce by one unit after each win. Every series is supposed to earn a profit, but there are times when your bets get so big, the only sensible option is to bail out and eat the loss.

The D'Alembert was designed to be played with a notepad, where you add numbers as you lose, and cross them out as you win. This keeps you in touch with where you are in the series, but I see no need for that if you obey your loss limits.

Analysis: there are better systems out there.

CONTRA-D'ALEMBERT: Here we have another mirror-image strategy, which, fortunately, has nothing to do with the Iran-Contra Affair or Honduras or any other banana republic. With the Contra-D'Alembert, you increase by one unit when you win, and decrease by one when you lose.

One positive aspect to this system is that when you hit a losing streak, the size of your bet is quickly reduced until it bottoms out at the one-unit level, which is where you stay until the wins return. This helps cover the downside, but trouble occurs when you hit a losing streak right after a winning streak, because if you stick to the system you'll give all your gains right back to the house. Therefore, it would make sense to get in the habit of leaving the table immediately after hitting a flurry of consecutive wins.

With that provision added in, this isn't a bad system, for it allows one to exploit favorable table conditions while holding down losses. But the elimination of one demon allows another to move to the front: should you encounter a wagering situation of wins that come in tight groups, one loss can blow away all your gains in a single stroke. For example:

Your first bet is one unit. You win and add a unit, so now you have a two-unit bet at risk. If that wins, your next wager is 3 units. Along comes your first loss and you have nothing to show for the fact that you won two of the last three decisions; all your profit was dissipated financing the wagering increases.

If such a trend was to persist, to continue would be suicide. You may never win a series.

One way to circumvent this little problem would be to use a three or more unit bet as your base, such as $15. When your first bet wins, your next bet is $20. Should that also win, you progress to $25. Then if you lose the third bet as you did in the first case, at least you'd have a two-unit profit.

At the right table, this system can work wonders. But that's the problem with systems: you gotta find the right table, and pick the right system, to use at the right point in time.

If I could do that, I wouldn't bother writing a book.

1-2-3-4 SYSTEM: The *1-2-3-4 System* is a four-stage progression that seeks to grab a win before the fourth stage of the series is reached. It's like a one-way pyramid: you start with a 1-unit bet, and progress to 2, 3 or 4 units—as required to win a series. Whether you win or lose the series, the idea is to regress to the one-unit level at its conclusion.

This is more of a procedure than a system, for it can be applied to even or non-even money bets, and, it doesn't pretend to show a profit at each stage. But I see it as one of the most basic procedures used by table game specialists, and regard its inclusion into the Systems category as a necessary part of your foundational training. What I'm saying, is that this system is the core of many viable table game procedures.

The 1-2-3-4 is not as drastic as the Martingale, for only ten units are risked throughout its four stages, as opposed to fifteen. Its strength lies in its moderation, for its soft increases do less potential damage to one's bankroll than the steep incline of the Martingale, and, the progression ends by the fourth stage. At a choppy table, the 1-2-3-4 is usually superior to flat bets.

But there's another way to utilize the 1-2-3-4. For bets that pay better than even money, there is a chance to show a profit at each stage of the progression. Such is the case with bets paying 9–5 and up. So, if the 1-2-3-4 was played against place bets at the craps table (for example), the 6–5, 7–5 and 9–5 bet returns might help you realize a profit at every stage.

OSCAR'S GRIND: This is the most conservative —and therefore perhaps the most viable—of all the systems shown in this chapter. Because it lacks ambition, it is the most ambitious strategy of them all.

One lousy unit. That's all you stand to win from each and every series. Not very exciting, but it does help you minimize your losses, which is 90% of successful gambling. Remember, more important than knowing how to *win* is knowing how to *not lose.* Oscar understands this.

The rules aren't *too* complicated:

1) Increase your bet by one unit after every win, provided it won't result in a series gain that exceeds one unit.
2) Never modify your bet size after a loss.

That's it. That's all you need to remember. Just follow those two rules and you can't miss.

Let's look at a hypothetical wagering example:

You lose your first six bets. Since your bet amount doesn't change following a loss, you are six units behind. Then you win one bet. Your next wager should be for [an increase of one] two units. If you should win that next bet as well, you go to a three-unit bet. If that one also wins, you'll be right where you started nine bets ago, even though you lost twice as many bets (six) as you won (three). But you still need a one-unit profit to end the series. Your next bet is just that: one unit. If it wins, the series is over and it's time to begin another one.

What you've just seen is, of course, an absolute best-case follow-up to a string of losses, but it was done without having to bring out any big guns. With the D'Alembert, six straight losses would put you twenty-one units behind, a far cry from six.

Although this system gets high ratings, it's not perfect. There are times when Oscar takes you to the land of large bets—but you'll do okay if you set up strict loss limits.

What could cause such a conservative system to fail? One thing would be solitary wins surrounded by multiple losses, on a continuing basis. This keep pushing your bet levels upward, and the only remedy is consecutive wins. If you should run into that, avoid resorting to large bets to pummel your way out of a bind. It's been done. By me, by everybody. And the lesson we learned is that it isn't worth it to sacrifice a week's worth of gains just to try to salvage one lousy session.

Having said that, just let me say that of all the systems I've seen, this one impresses me the most.

That must be why I saved it for last.

SUMMARY OF
SYSTEMS IN GAMING

*The game never ends when your whole world depends on
the turn of a friendly card.*
—The Alan Parsons Project

Like any other seasoned pro, I've seen fire and I've seen
rain. I've seen losing streaks that I thought would never end. I've
seen lonely times when I could not get a win. But I always
thought that the perfect system was out there. Somewhere.
Hidden by the trees, underneath a big stone, or maybe just too
friggin' obvious to see.

Forget about it. If it existed, I would have found it by now.
Trust me, I've checked every angle and analyzed a zillion
options eleventeen different ways. And I'm just one of many
fools throughout the centuries who have tried.

Anything can and will happen at the tables. No system can
cover every possibility. Some systems are better than others, but
the more successful it is, the greater the chance you'll encounter
a really big surprise right about the time you thought you were
finally safe. That's how it is, bro.

To be honest, I begrudge the space I used to show you
these systems, but I believe it's necessary. You need to know
these techniques because they are foundational. Sometimes I
have to refer to them in conveying similarities with a procedure
that *is* valid.

But mainly, as a gaming specialist, you can't afford to be
caught asking the question, *"What's a Martingale?"*

9

GAMING PROCEDURES

Now that we've passed through the land of systems, we are free to move to a higher plane. *Gaming procedures* are what you will be playing most of the time, and even though many players do the same, there is no grand design to what they do. That's what makes what you're doing better: while they're swimming in an ocean of cheap thrills and gluttony, you'll be walking through the stages of a master plan.

In this context, gaming *procedures* differ from gaming *systems* in that you will not be roboting through a frozen ritual. What you do will be structured, but you will be more sensitive to the permutations of the table.

Much of the time you may be making *surgical strikes,* which are isolated bets or progressions that are enacted only after a wagering trigger has been identified. Other times you'll jump into the stream of table decisions and do your best to swim with the current. In those cases, your objective will be to avoid being carried away by a riptide that is beyond your ability to control. But there will be times when that can't be helped. That's what makes gaming the challenge that it is.

SIZING UP THE TABLE

I learned early on: the more you know, the luckier you get.

—J. R. Ewing, from *Dallas*

Statistically, there are more *cold* than *warm* or *hot* craps tables in the world. This statement is just an acknowledgement of the probabilities, which reveal that all six of the point numbers are more likely *not* to pass, than to pass. So, if you're looking to cop a ride on the coattails of a streaking table, you should know how to play the side that wins the most.

Becoming a don't bettor, however, ain't the final answer. You may win more often, but your losses will be more dear. Possibly, enough to put you away for the night.

But if one must play both sides to succeed, how does he know which side to pick? Surely there's more to it than simply imitating the last table result?

Indeed there is, though winning at the tables is often little more than the product of a series of trial-and-error experiments. You may start out losing, in which case you must be cautious. Could turn out that you're at one of those weird tables that will never kick back a dime, ever. So, seek another table. Eventually, you'll find one that gives something back. Now, your focus is on how to make the most of the opportunity.

As you play, a picture will start to emerge. When the wins come automatically, you can bet with confidence. Other times, it will seem like you can't get a break.

Not a problem. Walk away and don't look back.

There are two outward signs you should be looking for: *warm* or *cold* table activity. Warm table activity is when the dice frequently pass, or place numbers are rolled in abundance on the way to a line decision. Cold table activity is when the 7 seems to be lurking behind every corner. Many craps tables incline toward one side or the other.

As it is in life, if you do your homework, you are better prepared to face whatever comes. Sizing up the table, beforehand and as you play, will keep you on track. Now, there is always the possibility that doing so will lead you straight into an ambush, but that's the exception, not the rule.

Information is all around us, all the time. Those who make use of it are the ones who stay on top.

BASIC LINE BETTING

Spare no expense to make everything as economical as possible.
—Attributed to Samuel Goldwyn

You want to hear a funny story? I once assembled all my old craps scorecards for a study. What would happen, I theorized, if I played basic line betting and nothing else? What if I simply followed the pattern, betting pass after shooters made the point, and don't pass after all the seven-outs? Would such a primal exploitation of gaming trends show a profit?

The bet parameters were elementary: on an ongoing basis, imitate the most recent line decision, and quit after the first loss that follows a profitable series of wins.

It looked very promising at first. . .but then I saw the flaw: whenever the table decisions zigzag, you'll do nothing but lose. So I added a rule that after three consecutive losses, discontinue play at that table. Amazingly, it worked.

You heard me. It worked! On paper, it overcame the house edge and showed a profit. Who knew it would be so simple?

Actually, it's not. My sampling was too small to assure any measure of scientific reliability. But it helps make the point that when playing a bet that has a minimal house edge, you just might make out okay doing nothing more than riding the streaks.

For those who seek a potential for gain with a minimum of planning and legwork, I would suggest basic line betting. Simply imitate the line decisions for as long as you continue to win. When you reach your win goal or when losses start to mount, go to another table, or quit for the day.

Doesn't *sound* hard, but some players actually cannot do it. Their problem is resisting the temptation to cover other numbers with place bets while a line decision is in progress. All around, they'll hear all the other players making "a ton of money" while they stand there waiting for a single decision.

Could you handle that?

Basic line betting was chosen as the first procedure to describe in this chapter because it is one of the staples of my wagering diet. I use it to 'tread water' at the table while pursuing another betting scheme like the *Sister System,* or placing inside numbers, or awaiting a lucrative hot or cold streak within the line bets themselves. While in the water-treading mode, my bets are frequently near the table minimum, and I often hedge during the come-outs. This involves playing any craps during come-outs when betting *right,* and hedging the Yo (11) when betting *wrong.* If I'm getting blasted by the 7 during back line come-outs, I resort to *odds betting* (the subject of the next subchapter), which brings all the nonsense to an immediate halt.

One word of caution: when exploitation of the table trends takes you to the back line, be prepared to deal with consecutive *naturals* during the come-out. Some players try to disregard them and eat the loss, but when you get burned by five or six in a row, it's real easy to lose control and get reckless.

Don't let that happen. Go straight to *odds betting.* That will keep you, not the table, in control.

ODDS BETTING

This is one of the most efficient bets you can play in a casino. With *odds betting* you can play both sides of the table without exposing yourself to the severe punishment that is frequently inflicted upon back line bettors during the come-out phase of the game.

Odds betting involves placing a bet on both the pass and the don't pass lines *simultaneously* at the come-out. This allows you to play the *odds* bet (with its 0% house edge) without having to go through the come-out gauntlet to get there. Once your man is on base, you put up the *odds* bet on the side of your choice. This concept was introduced by John Patrick, and is known as the *Patrick System* in his books on craps.

Playing pass and don't pass during the come-out may sound like betting on *red* and *black* simultaneously at the roulette table, but it's not at all the same. True, one cancels the other out, but *after* the point is established, you can play the best bet in the house as a tack-on to the foundation you've built. The only hang-up is the 12. If someone rolls one during the come-out, your bet on pass loses, but the don't pass bet is a push. With any other craps or natural roll, the one that loses is compensated by the one that wins. Not so with the 12 (which accounts for its .92% vig). Now, you could hedge with a small bet on the 12, but I usually do that only when betting large.

Once you're on base, follow the trend. If the last shooter made his point, bet *right*. If he sevened out, bet *wrong*. If you keep duplicating what last happened, you're in position to reap the bounty of any streak that might come along.

Some readers are sure to question why *basic line betting* is advocated if *odds betting* is so efficient. Truth to tell, line betting permits you to play to the trend more closely than odds betting. The latter eliminates the lows (very constructive, I agree) but it also takes out the highs. I once played a table where the shooter needed *nine rolls* to establish his point: 7–2–11–7–3–12–7–7–4! That's five naturals, three craps rolls and finally, the point. Since I was betting *right* and hedging every roll, his come-out gave me *eight* straight returns, which singlehandedly turned my session around. With odds betting, I would have just been turning over money for every one of those rolls, until losing outright to the 12 on the sixth roll.

Odds betting steals away gains from the don't side as well. If your table isn't showing a propensity for come-out sevens, you can get even money for your don't pass bets instead of paying the heavy penalty of laying $50 to win $25, as the case would be if the point was 4 or 10. Major difference.

But there's one more angle to consider. Serious gambling isn't pretty, or fun, or what most people imagine. Every so often, one needs a lift; a bonus; a present of some kind just to make it through the next fifteen minutes. You're not likely to get that with odds betting, which is as bland as anything you will ever experience. With line betting, these little bonuses fall into your lap from time to time, and buddy let me tell you that they can mean a lot to someone as emotionally deprived as a *disciplined* player of casino craps.

The upshot of all this is: odds betting is a terrific last resort; a way to shield yourself from the cruel downside that comes on like a storm and hangs on for what seems like forever. But there's no need to use it until it becomes necessary. Its purpose is to offer protection during the come-outs, but if you can manage without it, you'll save money.

And don't worry about what the dealer is going to think when he sees you betting both sides. By now, they've seen this technique enough times to take it in stride.

ADVANCED LINE BETTING

If you're properly prepared, you won't be easily surprised.

—Seen on a church marquee

What you have just read in the last four pages covers two ways of playing line bets at craps. It would be nice if you could pick one or the other and be done with it, but table patterns can fluctuate quickly. To maximize your gains, you need to alternate between the two, and then add in a third element. The resulting technique is what I call *advanced line betting.*

One of the problems that goes with following the trend at a craps table is the fact that the *do* side streaks tend to be shorter than the *don't* side streaks. At many tables, in fact, no one can make more than one point, if that. If you're imitating the last line decision, you can get beat up pretty bad at such a table if you are adding odds to your basic bet.

There's a way to cut way down on this expense.

If the last shooter made his point, but nobody seems to be making more than one, wait until after the point is established. Then, do one of two things: place the point, or, hold off from betting until that decision is known.

How do you know which one to pick? It's a judgment call. But either one will hold down your losses at tables where the *do* side streaks aren't happening.

If you choose to place the point, do it for the same amount as your pass line bet, *before* the odds are added. That will cut the cost of your investment in that shooter in half.

If you choose the *wait and see* approach, you might save even more money, but you also might miss the first opportunity to grab a *do* side win. Don't cry. Instead, use that as a signal that the trend is changing. After all, if he made two points, he might be good for more. Then again, it might just be a statistical blip. That's why I recommend that you stick to placing the point until you start accumulating some hard evidence.

I wish that was all there is to it, but there is one more angle to consider. What do you do when you're pausing your bets, and the shooter is rolling lots of naturals? Wouldn't that cause you to miss out on the best feature of the line bet?

True. But there's a way to handle that. It's a bit confusing for novices, but this is *advanced* line betting! What I do is make it a habit to revert back to line bets whenever the shooter starts out his roll with a natural. See, that's the tipoff that a string of naturals may be coming your way. But I recommend you hedge with any craps, because those extended come-outs usually have a craps roll or two mixed in with the good stuff.

In those cases, do you continue to shun the odds bet? This is your call, but that decision should be shaped by the past table patterns, and where you stand monetarily.

The following is a summary of *advanced line betting:*

At a craps table, wait to see two consecutive passes or two seven-outs. That's your cue to begin, and you do so by playing whichever (line bet) side won those last two. I recommend small hedges on the any craps for the *do* side, and the yo when playing the back line, but these are optional. Continue to follow the trend by imitating the last line result.

If you get burned by short *do* streaks, revert to place bets, or hold back, as noted above.

If you get burned at the come-out by the 7 while playing the *don't* side, go to odds betting until the trend dissipates. Later, you can reinstate the don't pass bets. And if you hit a super-cold trend, you might be able to get more from the table by launching the *two-number don't,* coming up.

Finally: if you keep losing, wise up. Get on out of there!

THE TWO-NUMBER DON'T

When playing follow the leader with line bets, there will be times when you hit a trend that's cold enough to make you blue! Sure, you're making money, but you could be making quite a bit more if you covered more numbers. In those cases, there's not a reason in the world why you shouldn't!

The *two-number don't* is a betting procedure that involves betting don't pass, and immediately after, *one* don't come bet. This helps maximize your potential for gain at a cold table by giving you more coverage, and spreading the risk.

At a new (line bet) come-out, drop $10 on the *don't pass.* Let's say that 9 becomes the point, so you lay $15 odds and then drop $10 into the *don't come.* Now the shooter rolls a 4, so that bet goes behind the 4. Then you pull your odds off your basic don't pass bet and await the decision.

At a cold table, this may be the most efficient universal strategy you can use. Through precision timing and moderation, you've conscripted the almighty 7, without the usual penalty associated with laying numbers. If the cold trend holds up and the timing doesn't blow up in your face, this technique will allow you to get an even money return while you maintain a statistical wagering advantage.

That's not a bad place to be.

Most don't come bettors play two or more bets per come-out, while some like to play a continuous chain. That is precisely the trap that you would do well to avoid. The two-number don't is a more conservative way to play, but I believe it maximizes the back line potential.

Betting the don't pass *only* has limitations. For one thing, those bets can't win from a come-out seven like the (established) don't come bets, which are out of sync with the line decisions. This helps you make use of *all* the sevens. Playing more than one don't come bet, however, pushes the productivity envelope, for the bets entering the come-out will at some point fall to the line bet seven-outs that come sooner than you'd like. In that case, they drain the profit out of the bets that win. You're better off if you don't overplay the seven card.

At a cold table, you may do nothing but win with this procedure. At most choppy tables and even some warm tables, you can also do well, for you don't necessarily need a seven-out to win. But you'll be able to take advantage of the fact that most table decisions, in fact, end with a seven-out.

Perhaps the best feature of this procedure, though, is how the two bets draw strength from each other's presence. As soon as you get your don't pass wager on board, you can add odds, which act as a shield to protect the don't come bet you are now about to make. Should the seven-out come immediately, the odds offset the loss of the DC bet that got burned in the come-out. Once that bet is safely on board, though, you remove those costly odds, and enjoy the advantage you now hold: two chances to get an even money return while you retain a better-than-even-chance to win *both* of those bets.

For maximum efficiency, it's best that you start out 'treading water' with line bets until the table tips its hand. Once you have determined that a table truly is cold, add in the don't come phase, but keep a close watch on both bets. Put your emphasis on the ones that win, and increase your bet size as the profits come in. And if you hit an extended winning streak, leave after the first loss that follows that run. Don't give all your gains back to the house!

Most important, don't try to make the two-number don't work at a warm table, thinking that the trend is bound to change. If you keep losing, get a clue. There are lots of other tables. Chances are, there's something better out there.

$22 INSIDE
AND OTHER MULTIPLE PLACE BETS

When the table starts heating up, or, when you see a pattern where lots of numbers are rolled between come-outs, it may be time for *$22 Inside,* or a variation thereof.

We're talking *place* bets, which should remain in action for only a short time. Their purpose is to help the player capitalize on warm spells at the craps table.

$22 inside is the command to the craps dealer to *place* the four *inside* numbers (5, 6, 8 & 9). Statistically, they are the most frequently-rolled numbers at the craps table—after the 7. When you cover those four, you have exactly *half* of the thirty-six dice combinations working for you. The only catch is that one little seven will knock them all down.

This book advocates placing numbers in groups only when the table is sending the right signals, and then, only for short periods. It can be a tough loss to bear, especially when one plays larger multiples of the $22 base amount.

To play this group of bets successfully, you need to get in the habit of calling those bets *off,* or taking them down, after you've gotten two, three, or perhaps four hits—whatever you think you can get away with. Then keep them down until the next shooter comes up to the plate. Now, if you play this group of bets, there will be many times when you'll get scorched by the seven on the very first roll after you put them up. Playing daredevil with the seven is seldom easy, but if you can get the hang of it, you might discover there's some good money to be made here. Just don't forget what a precarious ledge it is upon which those sitting ducks sit.

The breakdown of the $22 inside wager is as follows: $5 each on the 5 & 9, and $6 each on the 6 & 8. Remember, the 6 & the 8 must each be placed in $6 increments (see Chapter 5). Together, the four bets add up to $22.

In all honesty, there shouldn't be that much call for you to ever play $22 inside *specifically,* or even a multiple thereof. Much of the time you'll have one of the four numbers covered (more efficiently) with your *pass line + odds* wagers, in which case you will decline coverage of the number that happens to be the point. If 9 was the point and you wanted coverage on the (remaining) inside numbers, for example, you would request *$17 inside,* because that's how much the other three cost at the $5 level. And if 8 was the point, you'd ask for *$16 inside,* because one of the $6 bets (the point of 8) would not need coverage as in the previous example. Since most players bet the pass line, dealers know exactly what you want when you ask for off-amounts like $16 or $17 inside.

As if this wasn't already confusing enough, we must now address the matter of *outside bets,* which happen to be personal favorites of mine.

Now, don't be blaming me for this, but it's a fact that there's some overlay between the *inside* and *outside* bets. Generally, *inside* bets mean 5, 6, 8 & 9, and usually, *outside* bets mean 4, 5, 9 & 10. See the problem? The 5 & 9 swing both ways. But it gets worse. The term *outside bets* can also mean just the pairing of the 4 & 10, so there will be times when the dealer won't be sure exactly what you want. Usually, he can figure it out from context, or from your prior wagering patterns. But it would be a good idea to be prepared to tell him what you mean in specific terms if he should ask.

Why bother with *outside* bets? Well, sometimes the table can favor those numbers, and since they (as a group) pay better than the *inside* numbers (as a group), it might serve you well to pay attention to such inclinations. Hey, it won't do much good to cover the 6 & 8 if those numbers aren't hitting. Remember, *playing to the trend* is how you win.

Apart from letting you know about these betting options, the purpose of this lesson is to tune you in to the nomenclature you'll need to know in the various wagering situations you'll encounter. For example, if the point is 5 and you wish to cover the remaining outside numbers at the one-unit level, you toss $15 on the layout and say, *"$15 outside, please."* The dealer would assume that you mean the non-point numbers, since there is no way to evenly divide $15 between just the 4 and 10.

Sometimes the table minimum will clarify what you want. At a $5 table, *"$20 outside"* would probably get you coverage on the four outside numbers (unless you specify otherwise). But if that table had a $10 minimum, the same request would put coverage on just the 4 and 10, because the $20 you laid down was sufficient to cover only two numbers.

Now we come to betting the place numbers *across.* At a craps table, this means either covering all six place numbers, or, covering all those *except* for the point. For this set of wagers, there is no chance the dealer will confuse your intent (as long as you give him the correct amount), because the two sets of figures can each be applied only one way.

There's just one more matter we need to address: *buy* bets. When betting the 4 or 10 at the $25 level, it's more economical to *buy* the number than to *place* it. This was covered in Chapter 5 and is demonstrated in figs. 21 and 22, but we need to mention this now, because it affects the size of the group wager. As a general rule, for every $25 wagered on a buy bet, add $1 to cover the house commission, which you'll gladly pay for the privilege of getting the better deal.

Now, before you go charging on out there putting up a wall of bets, you need a sign that the table is ripe. I generally wait until one of the inside numbers hits before putting up place bets, and they are added cautiously; one or two at a time.

The real art in placing bets in groups like these lies in being sensitive to the inclinations of the table. In time, you will learn when to advance, and when to retreat.

If not, better not spend too much time in a casino!

TABLE STATUS | VERBAL COMMAND

When 8 is the point:

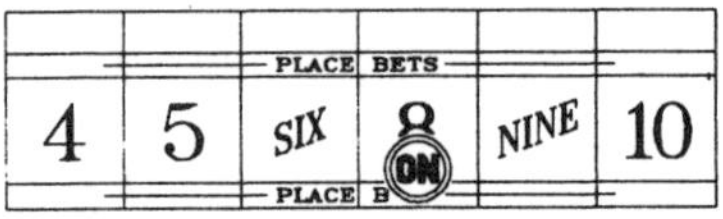
PLACE BETS
4
5
SIX
8
ON
NINE
10
PLACE B

"$16 inside."
COVERS THE THREE NON-POINT INSIDE NUMBERS

"$20 outside."
COVERS THE FOUR OUTSIDE NUMBERS

"$26 across."
COVERS ALL NUMBERS EXCEPT THE POINT

When 9 is the point:

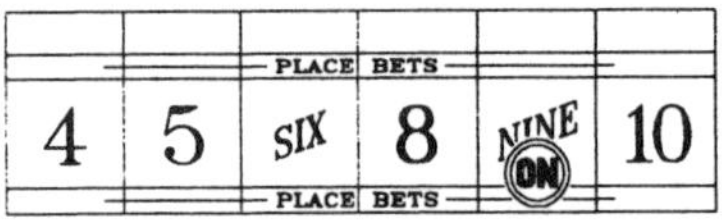
PLACE BETS
4
5
SIX
8
NINE
ON
10
PLACE BETS

"$17 inside."
COVERS THE THREE NON-POINT INSIDE NUMBERS

"$15 outside."
COVERS THE THREE NON-POINT OUTSIDE NUMBERS

"$27 across."
COVERS ALL NUMBERS EXCEPT THE POINT

When 10 is the point:

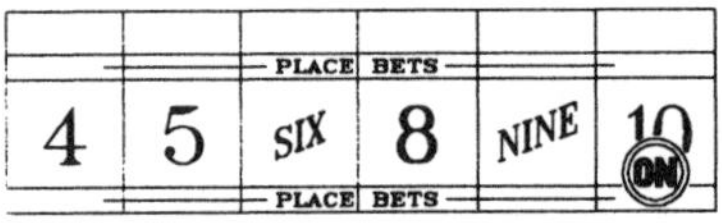
PLACE BETS
4
5
SIX
8
NINE
10
ON
PLACE BETS

"$22 inside."
COVERS ALL INSIDE NUMBERS

"$15 outside."
COVERS THE THREE NON-POINT OUTSIDE NUMBERS

"$32 across."
COVERS ALL SIX NUMBERS

FIGURE 21
Nomenclature for Multiple Place Bets

	1 unit coverage	2 unit coverage	5 unit coverage
WHEN 6 IS THE POINT	***$16 inside*** ***$20 outside*** ***$26 across***	***$32 inside*** ***$40 outside*** ***$52 across***	***$80 inside*** ***$102 outside*** ***$132 across***
WHEN 5 IS THE POINT	***$17 inside*** ***$15 outside*** ***$27 across***	***$34 inside*** ***$30 outside*** ***$54 across***	***$85 inside*** ***$77 outside*** ***$137 across***
WHEN 4 IS THE POINT	***$22 inside*** ***$15 outside*** ***$27 across***	***$44 inside*** ***$30 outside*** ***$54 across***	***$110 inside*** ***$76 outside*** ***$136 across***

FIGURE 22
Nomenclature for Place Bets
(Different Coverage Amounts)

CLOSED PROGRESSIONS

"You caught that right on the last stage of the progression, didn't you?" said the craps dealer as he made the payoff for my successful place bet on the 5.

"Yeah," I agreed, though a little surprised at the unsolicited remark. Seldom do you get comments like that from a craps dealer. But this was in 1992, at the time of the culinary workers' strike at the Frontier in Vegas, and during that period it seemed like there were a lot of strange things going on there.

Didn't matter to me. Back then, I couldn't lose no matter what I did in that casino. (Looking back, it's safe to say that, but switching to the present tense and saying, *"I can't lose in that casino"* would certainly and absolutely put the kiss of death on any winning streak of mine.)

At the time, I was playing a *closed progression* (on the 5) at one of the Frontier's warm tables, during a winning period I was blessed with at the time. The progression I played cost $55 per series, and was structured as shown:

LEVEL	BET	COST	WIN	PROFIT *(at that stage)*
1	$5	$5	$7	$7
2	$10	$15	$14	$9
3	$15	$30	$21	$6
4	$25	$55	$35	$5

FIGURE 23
Progression On The 5

Let's say you're going to play a progression on the 5 at two different craps tables. You are seeking out two warm tables (one at a time), and your win goal is $50 at each, which would get you to your win goal of $100 for the day. To achieve this, you're willing to risk $55 for each session.

At level 1 from Figure 23, you're risking $5 in your attempt to make $7. At level 2, your $10 bet (if successful) will recoup your previous loss, *and* return a $9 profit. At level 3, you stand to win $6 after paying for the two prior losses. At level 4, you're risking $25 more to make a series profit of $5. If four tries don't get it, you leave the table with $55 less than when you arrived, unless you had some wins along the way.

If your table stays warm, you are more likely to win $50 than lose the $55 session money. If not, there would be a fair chance that you won close to $50 before suffering a series loss. All you're seeking is enough wins to earn $50 before leaving, which works out to between six and ten wins.

What I have just described is a four-stage progression utilizing soft increases, on a wager that pays slightly better than even money (7–5, to be exact). The bet is *placing* the number 5 at a craps table, though one might prefer placing the 9 (which has the same return), if that number is making its presence known in a conspicuous fashion.

Now, before initiating play with this system, be sure to wait until the chosen wagering target hits before sending your man out into the battle zone. Yes, this means you're going to miss what *would have been a win,* but doing so will undoubtedly save your ass countless times from shooters who establish the point and then seven-out on the very next roll.

Closed progressions such as this one have their strong points, but they are far from infallible. At a warm table, they'll quickly get you to your win goal, but you could get burned if your table suddenly turns cold. This book does advocate closed progressions, but this advice applies only to those who have found a way to make them work. If you're having difficulty, concentrate your efforts elsewhere.

THE SISTER SYSTEM

Back in Chapter 5 (page 45) you were told about sister numbers as they applied to a pair of dice. The most significant are the three groupings: 6+8, 5+9, and 4+10, for they are the only numbers that may be wagered as place bets.

Despite its name, the *sister system* is actually not a system. It is a targeting procedure for *sister numbers* on a pair of dice, that was inspired by an observation I once made: that the sister number to any given point number frequently comes up on the way to a line decision.

This struck me as an opportunity. I reasoned that I could place bet the sister, and then take the bet down after getting a hit. It wouldn't matter if the shooter made his point or not. My profit would be made. This, therefore, appeared to be a more reliable wagering target than the point itself.

Ultimately, I was smacked in the face by the reality that *some tables do and some don't*. I added a provision that you wait until seeing a *would-be win* go by, then launch a progression. That configuration was the procedure known as the *sister system* in the original version of this book.

That strategy, however, was missing an important element: As a *do* side strategy, it disregarded the opportunities that exist on the *don't* side, for I have found that some tables produce long stretches where the sister is absent.

What follows is a reconfigured strategy, which is designed to take advantage of the streaks that are common on both sides of the table, as they pertain to sister numbers.

ALTHOUGH I prefer playing this strategy as a *surgical strike,* which is covered in the next chapter, there are times when a table trend is so pervasive that you can rack up a considerable number of consecutive wins by simply imitating the last result. That is, doing whatever would have last produced a win. But you need to take a little time to see what's going on at your table before you commit yourself to one side or the other. If you're not seeing any major opportunities (on either side) going by, hold off on betting until you see something good. Then, pick the side that's winning and put down your bet.

One reason this was originally created as a front line procedure is the dilemma one faces, laying against the 4 and 10. In those cases, you'll be laying two units, plus the commission, to win one. Thus, it requires more than two wins to make up for a single loss. That never sat well with me.

At that juncture, you have four options:

1) Lay the 5 or 9 instead;
2) Switch to the *do* side for that bet;
3) Sit out all the 4 & 10 decisions, or
4) Go ahead and pay those heavy odds.

In trying to determine which of the four options to choose, you need to think about the history of that table. If you're seeing a lot of quick seven-outs, I'd go with option one: it might get the same result, with less potential liability. If the table is choppy, a small *do* side bet might be best. If your session is not going well, I'd recommend sitting it out. And if your lay bets are winning, I would be tempted to take door number four.

As for laying the 5 or 9: I'm not crazy about paying those penalties, either, but they're tolerable.

Some players won't like laying the 6 or 8, because of their high win rate. But some tables go for remarkably long stretches without any playable sixes or eights. Never forget: *the back line is the side that wins the most.*

The sister system is not a bad strategy, for it helps you pace your wagering. And that's a good cause.

MULTI-LINE

This procedure is more suitable for readers who are already familiar with the game of craps. It's not complicated, but I can see how it would *appear* to be, to a newcomer.

I've never been very fond of come bets, because I feel they are addictive, and therefore dangerous. But years ago it came to my attention that a single come bet makes a terrific complement to line bets, when playing both sides. The essence of *Multi-Line* is to follow the trend, imitating the most recent line bet result (pass or don't pass), then add one come bet once the point is established. Now you have three types of bets working for you, though never more than two *types* at the same time.

Then, all you do is cater your play to the current trend. How do you do that? Analyze the effectiveness of your bets as you play. Increase or reduce certain bets. Add or forego the odds. Put your emphasis on the bets that win.

There are just two particulars you need to know. First, you play come bets only; never the don't come. See, half the value of the come bet is to hedge the possibility of a seven-out right after the line bet point is established. To a come bet, it's a come-out seven. Second, never let more than two come bets accumulate. If you have two active come bets up, avoid adding more until a decision against at least one of them occurs.

If it serves your purpose to use the come bet primarily as a hedge, by all means play it that way. This means foregoing odds, so that the bet size of your 'hedge' represents a larger percentage of your active wagers, as a group.

That's all there is to it. Just keep on top of things.

THE DOUBLE EVEN

The *Double Even* is a procedure for craps that came to me while playing online. After looking over some scorecards I had accumulated, I noticed that when two of the even point numbers (4, 6, 8 & 10) are rolled during any come-out, a third number from that group is often not far behind.

Of course, all table decisions are independent results, so I am not trying to say that this third number is induced by the table pattern that preceded it. But I've found that two even numbers in a single come-out can make a good wagering trigger.

Why? It usually takes several rolls for this pattern to show up, so the shooter (in many cases) has proven that he has some lasting power. That counts for something.

To get maximum efficiency, however, I suggest that it is played a certain way: what you're looking for is a number from the 6 & 8 group, and then one more from the 4 & 10 group, to be rolled during the same come-out. Then you place the two other numbers that *weren't* rolled. The series ends when you get a hit (from either number), or the come-out ends (without a decision), or you lose your bets to a 7. When one of those occurs, wait for a new trigger before launching another series.

Two things you should know about this:

1) The point, if it happens to be an even number, counts as the first of the two numbers you're looking for.

2) This procedure, played exclusively, will ultimately fail. It's a neat little trick, but not infallible. If you lose two in a row at a table, turn your attention elsewhere.

AUXILIARY BETS

As a serious player, your success rate may depend on your ability to recognize a conspicuous trend and catch a piece of it before it fades. But frequently you will be committed to another procedure when this observation is made, posing a dilemma: *Where doth exist the line between pursuing an opportunity, and abandoning one's discipline?*

Example: you're playing the *sister system* at craps, which commits you to cover just *one* number, when you realize that everyone's rolling a lot of numbers on the way to a line decision. You would like to cover some inside numbers to take advantage of this, but doing so messes up the accounting for your strategy. And anyway, wouldn't that be in conflict with the discipline you're sworn to uphold?

There is a way to handle this problem: *Auxiliary Bets.* Bets that are made from a separate fund that has been assembled solely for that purpose. But this fund should be smaller than your original buy-in, and closely monitored.

In the above example, you would make a secondary buy-in, even if you could afford them from your rack, because you want the monies to be *separate.* This fund should be no greater than 30% of your original buy-in. Then be sure to keep track of how these new bets are doing.

If you don't see positive results almost immediately, you might be ahead to acknowledge that it was not the opportunity you thought it was, and get back to what you were involved with before this distraction came along.

Auxiliaries are designed to serve you, not vice versa.

SUMMARY OF
GAMING PROCEDURES

In gaming, the difference between *systems* and *procedures* is that the former are close-ended strategies that have a *do-or-die* mentality. They work *most* of the time, but when they fail, you're left with an expensive mess to clean up.

Gaming *procedures* do not aspire to such a lofty goal. They are like tools in one's toolkit. For this table, you need a hammer. For that one, you need the wrench. The seasoned player succeeds because he takes the time to evaluate the table, then pick the right tool for the job.

Some table game experts specialize in certain procedures, like playing the back line at craps or even money bets at roulette. In those cases, they don't need to carry many tools. But most pros like to keep their options open toward several games so they're ready for almost anything.

Although the serious players thrive upon the anomalies of gaming, they must take care not to become ensnarled in one that happens to turn against them. In this business, bull-headedness can be fatal to one's wallet. If you are unable to get the result you seek, accept the fact that that item is out of stock *at that table*. Go elsewhere. Trying to force the result is more likely to destroy you than make you rich. It would be ironic to be undone by that which brought you riches in the first place.

Wouldn't it?

Make the most of the offering. A table, like money, makes an excellent servant, but a terrible master.

10

SURGICAL STRIKES

I take my luck where I find it.

—Gregory Peck
The World in His Arms

As I understand it, a *surgical strike* is *an offensive maneuver that endeavors to strike an enemy target with pinpoint precision.* Through coordination of timing and position, one of two warring sides hopes to hit a precise target and nothing more, then exit quickly before the enemy can react.

That sounds a lot like what you'll be doing in casinos, if you follow the advice of this book. Over a period of time you'll size up the table while calculating which weapon would be the most effective. When your evaluation is complete, you'll send in a 'smart bomb' to hit the assigned target. Whether your strike is successful or not, your next move is to head straight for the door. There is no way the table is going to lure you into prolonging the engagement.

In this book, the terms *surgical strike* and *one-shot* are synonymous. Officially, these terms describe a single wager that begins and ends a session, but there is also an informal version that is comprised of a brief wagering series. In this chapter we will take a look at both interpretations.

129

THE APPLICATION OF RACETRACK WAGERING TECHNIQUES TO CASINO GAMES

To win, you have to play the odds; but sometimes it pays to play a longshot.
—the Author

At some point in my career development, I came up with a neat little trick that helped me out many times. Whenever my losses began to mount, I often resorted to *one-shots*. These were large solo wagers made randomly at table games, after the disposition of the table had been assessed for specific trends. These were really just bail-out bets.

An example would be to walk up to a craps table and look it over. If the place and come areas are loaded with chips and the players are enthusiastic, you may have found a warm table. The point is 10 and you've watched at least three rolls go by. When you can get the dealer's attention, you drop $105 on the layout and say, *"Buy the point for a hundred."*

The dealer will give the money to the boxman, then pull out four greens and stack them in the 10 box, with a *buy* button on top. At this point you're hoping a 10 will be rolled before a 7. Only those two numbers can affect your bet.

A decision is likely in the next few minutes. If you win, have the dealer take down your bet *("Down on my buy, please"),* and he'll probably give you twelve greens. Collect your $195 profit at the cashier window, then take a break.

I want to emphasize that this tactic is NOT recommended to correct a losing binge, for it was conceived from a desperate need to compensate losses. It was surprisingly effective when it worked (which seemed often enough), but the price I paid for victory was a lapse in my discipline, too dear a cost. But its effectiveness led to an observation.

I began to compare casino wagers with those at racetracks, and realized that casinos offer many advantages if you pretend you're at the track instead. (This assumes you're there for the money, not the entertainment.) Look at it this way: at the track, let's say the favorite is 7–5 odds at post time. There are ten other horses in the field, and longshots *do* occasionally win. You have one way to win and ten ways to lose.

Not very good odds for a bet that pays only slightly better than even money.

The favorite is most likely to win, but if today happens to be a longshot day (those flukes of nature when the favorites lose, all day long), you could end up spending Saturday night pulling harpoons out of your butt.

At a craps table you can get the same 7–5 odds placing the 9, with just *one way* to lose. Or bet *against* the 9 (which pays less), but you'll still have just *one way* to lose.

Statistically, a bet on the 9 will lose more often than win, but when looked at as a one-shot deal at a fresh table, you have a 50-50 chance no matter which side you pick. But there's another matter to consider: the 15% to 30% house edge that goes with all racetrack wagers. Whatever that figure is at your local track, that's the percentage of your bets that will *lose* as a consequence of the "tax" imposed by the track.

In sharp contrast, the house edge for a place bet on the 9 is just 4%. This figure also applies to the sister number, the 5, and, the house penalty for placing the 6 or the 8 is just 1.52 %. Under 2 %!

This struck me as a much better deal, provided that a racetrack situation could be simulated in a casino.

Welcome to the concept of *Imposed Velocity.*

IMPOSED VELOCITY: As noted in the pages describing *Continuum,* the problem with casinos is that they make you play too darn fast. But, do they really?

Actually, no. That's what they encourage, and they don't mind you thinking that, but the pace can be whatever you want if you plan ahead. There is no need to play the way *they* want; you can opt to *impose your own playing velocity.*

This is how to merge the best of both worlds.

It may help you achieve the proper mentality by pretending, when in a casino, that you're at a racetrack instead:

You walk up to a craps table. *They're all in line. . .the flag is up, aaand, they're off!*

You reach into your pocket for a bill. *Coming around the clubhouse turn, it's. . .*

You tell the dealer your bet. . .*on the backstretch, Asian Cat has moved into contention. . .*

The shooter throws the dice. . .*aaaand at the top of the stretch, Asian Cat has taken the lead!*

The stickman calls, *"Number 9, winner!"* as the racetrack announcer says, *And it's number nine, Asian Cat, by two lengths, followed by the seven. . . .*

The dealer pays your bet and you head for the cashier.

The utilization of *imposed velocity* helps keep you from getting pulled in to the continuum the casinos rely on to guarantee their profits. *You* are the one controlling the pace of the betting activity instead of the casino.

What you now have is a simulation of racetrack conditions without the destructive 20% house edge. You can turn over money at a pace *you* choose, and give yourself the time you need to make an intelligent wagering decision. All that's missing is watching the horses run around the track.

That's not why you go, is it?

But there is one more little twist. This is most effective when you add in the mentality of *Controlled Greed.*

CONTROLLED GREED: During perhaps the most compelling moment of the movie *Wall Street,* Gordon Gekko echoed the words of takeover specialist Ivan Boesky, who once proclaimed that *Greed is good.* In that context, Mr. Gekko was right, but greed is also the great destroyer of men who were legends, and some of the most brilliant minds in world history. It is considered a deadly sin by most everyone—myself included— but it has it's place, if controlled.

Controlled greed? Greed used moderately? Yep. This is just one of the many paradoxes of gaming. All the same, it would be advantageous for you to introduce the concept of *controlled greed* into your style of play.

To survive as a successful gambler, one needs an excess of ambition and a touch of greed. You have to have the stomach for large bets, but also the good sense to quit at the right moment. You must desensitize yourself to the large sums of money you're turning over, while you retain the underlying knowledge of how much those chips are worth.

Controlled Greed is *a passionate desire for a sensible bet acquisition.* In this application, *greed* is constructive, for it offers the motivation to carry you through the gratification vacuum that is frequently part of this life.

You need an incentive to guide you past the temptations and the loneliness that constantly surround you. You will be in the no-man's land between *seduction* and *discipline.* There will be no peace until you're finished for the day.

Until you've been there, you can't begin to imagine what lies ahead. Sorry, you can't do it. You have to pay the dues and make the moves. And if you're anything like the rest of us humans on planet earth, you're going to have to make the same mistake ten thousand times before you've learned enough to stay out of trouble for one week. Did I say ten thousand? I meant twenty thousand.

With the help of this book, it should be easier for you than it was for me, but it's important that you stick to all the rules, right down to the tiniest detail.

APPLYING THE CONCEPTS

How are these concepts of *imposed velocity* and *controlled greed* applied in real life?

You have to know what to look for, and stay focused. The first stage as you enter a casino is the *Analysis Stage*. What's the general mood? Is there enough room at the tables? Any trends in progress? You're a shopper, looking for a bargain that may be hidden underneath a bunch of old crates.

As the situation comes into focus, you mentally prepare for the bets you will make, including how much cash to put on the table, what to say and—most important—when to leave. At that point, your role has changed from that of a shopper, to a Marine Corps General in charge of a small war.

The assignment is to *seize, retain, and exploit the initiative.* Before you send a single soldier (dollar) to engage the enemy (the house), you must possess a razor-sharp vision of exactly how that battle will end. You must visualize victory, and defeat. You must follow through on your attack regardless the result. This is a limited war in which no more will be risked than what you decided upon at the front end. There is no chance you'll be surprised, or drawn into a war of attrition. You'll be out of there in a matter of minutes.

Your goals are conservative. You're not after a lucky win. There are only two possible outcomes, and you have sized up the parameters of each. This is where you need your discipline. This is where you'll find out if you have the right stuff. This is where you just might discover what you can do.

SURGICAL ONE-SHOTS

Whenever I buy in for a craps session, my goal is to win a majority of small bets. Not so with the *one-shots.* Since they are fewer in number, more precise, and since I have more time to analyze the table, they are usually larger.

THE RANDOM 22

Moving in silently, downwind and out of sight, you've got to strike when the moment is right, without thinking.

—Pink Floyd, from
Animals

The *Random 22* is a technique every craps player should know about. It's a cluster of four separate wagers that is usually played sporadically as an ongoing strategy. It is advisable to play this only at *warm* craps tables.

With *$22 Inside,* you are covering each of the four inside numbers (5, 6, 8 & 9) with one-unit place bets. Since these four can be rolled a total of eighteen ways, you are covering exactly *half* of the total dice combinations. This sounds pretty good when one considers that these bets can win indefinitely.

The downside is that while you *win* your bets one at a time, you *lose* them all at once. So, anyone who plays this strategy must forever play dodge ball with the 7.

That sounds a bit like playing Russian Roulette for a living. That 7 is a straight shooter who never runs out of ammo. But at the right table, one can do remarkable things with this strategy. Just remember to watch yourself.

It might help you understand this cat-and-mouse procedure if I describe my first two experiences:

My first session was at the Flamingo Hilton in Las Vegas, where I made $200 in about forty minutes playing at the two-unit level (which costs $44, not $22). I was doing my best to artfully dodge the 7 by taking my bets down after three hits per shooter, but doing so hurt more than helped. You see, the table was warm to the point that I'd have made more if I left my bets up *until the 7 took them down*. That's what the other players did, and they were doing better than me. In that case, my discipline was in fact a liability—but please, don't even *think* about using that as an argument against maintaining your discipline!

My next session was next door at the Imperial Palace. I was at another warm table, doing quite well using my instinct to call my bets *off* and *on* at random. I was roughly $150 ahead when I got burned and lost my first $44. Then I fell into a loop where the 7 came the instant I called my bets *on*. I tried a series of counting procedures to compensate, but it mattered not. The 7 was *right there* every time I activated my bets.

The moral to story one is that a right bettor can do no wrong at a warm table. The moral to story two is that when the 7 starts blasting your bets off the board, Get out! Get out! Get out! Now! Now! Now!

The *Random 22* is generally most effective when one limits himself to two or three hits, then pulls down all bets until the next come-out, or the next table. At the right table, you can rack up some wins pretty quick.

The only problem is, those tables aren't all that abundant in the world.

THE RANDOM BUY

Attain the unattainable.

—Alfred Lord Tennyson

There was just one player at the table, and his point was 10. Even though the situation didn't meet my usual criterion for betting, I decided to risk $52 on a hunch. I took two greens and two whites from my pocket, put them on the layout near the dealer and said, *"Buy the point for fifty."* After about one minute I won $100. As I was wondering what to do next, the shooter came out on the 4. I decided to invest in him one more time, regressing my bet to $25 (+$1 for the commission). He made that point as well.

For the third point that I was there to see, he came out on 9. My original instinct was to place the point for a quarter, but a voice inside my head said that since it was easy for the shooter to make the two hardest points, 4 and 10, it might be difficult for him to make an easier point like the 9. I held back, but stuck around long enough to see the result. After two more rolls, he sevened out. My bottom line was a net gain of $147 in just under five minutes—from an initial investment of $52.

This happened some years ago at the Resorts in Atlantic City. What I did was *buy the 10,* and later, the 4. I prefer to take that kind of risk only at warm tables, but sometimes one can do well operating strictly from instinct.

So, what you should really be seeking is a *lively* craps table where the point is 4 or 10. And the more excited the players seem to be, the more eager you should be to *buy the point,* if you can manage to squeeze in.

If, however, the players seem disinterested and bored, you're better off avoiding that table altogether. And if you're wondering, I don't recommend laying the point. Just keep on walking. When you're in the *Random Buy* mode, you're looking for a hot chance on a 2–1 bet or no bet at all.

Now, technically, this bet doesn't pay 2–1 because a 5% commission is levied by the house. But there are times when you pay less than that through rounding.

Fig. 24 shows some common buy bets, which are advisable only with the numbers 4 and/or 10:

BET	COMMISSION		TOTAL BET	WIN	PROFIT
$ 20	$1	(5%)	$ 21	$ 40	$ 39
$ 25	$1	(4%)	$ 26	$ 50	$ 49
$ 35	$1	(2.9%)	$ 36	$ 70	$ 69
$ 50	$2	(4%)	$ 52	$100	$ 98
$100	$5	(5%)	$105	$200	$195

FIGURE 24
Buying the 4 or 10

Note that when buying the 4 or 10 for $25, you pay only a 4% commission. When buying for $35, you pay less than 3%. This is called the miracle of numerical rounding. Many casinos, in an attempt to make the bet more attractive, allow the 5 percent figure to be rounded *downward.* Some other casinos, however, accept house commissions in fifty-cent increments, in which case some of the above figures may not apply.

Now, I don't want to paint a rosy picture. The hard truth is this isn't an easy bet to win. If that wasn't the case, the boxman wouldn't accept your bet so gleefully. See, the man isn't stupid. He knows that for every 4 or 10 that wins, two will lose. That's the probability, Jack.

Nevertheless, if you restrict your play to when the table is exhibiting signs of warmth, there's a chance you can beat the odds. You'll never know until you try.

THE RANDOM LAY

Everything in life, it seems, is a trade-off. If it tastes good, it's probably bad for your system. In matters of love, you often have to choose between stunning looks and a loving heart. If you like living in a city that offers everything you could want, you must endure a higher crime rate.

The same rules apply in gaming. If you seek a greater quantity of wins, you must settle for a low return.

Such is the case for those who prefer to back the 7 at craps. The odds are on their side, but they get beat up pretty bad when they lose.

If you happen to sidle up to a table that has only a handful of grim-looking players whose chip racks are nearly empty and some of them are betting the back line, chances are pretty good you've found a *cold table*. One way to handle that situation is to lay the point immediately, then continue to do so as long as you keep winning. Using the base level *lay bet* cost figures shown in Figure 17 (page 62), you just might be able to squeeze out five or ten or more consecutive victories.

Riding a wave of consecutive wins is not too hard to learn. The real art lies in reading the table signs beforehand. One thing that has helped me immeasurably in the past is to ask the closest player how the table's running. The answer often surprises me. When it does, I hold back as I await evidence to confirm or deny that appraisal. Of course, table trends can change directions in a heartbeat, especially at craps.

As you continue to win, lay each new point until you lose. Then, hold back or reduce your bet as you await the next outcome. If you lose again, it's time to take a hike.

THE RANDOM LAY: VERSION TWO

For all its simplicity, the *random lay: version two* can be remarkably effective. It is essentially a clone of the *random lay,* but the betting trigger is more precise.

The best 'platform' for playing this strategy is a casino that has numerous active craps tables. Being in an area with multiple casinos would be even more helpful.

Here's what you do: Go up to an active table and wait for a seven-out. Then you lay the next established point. Win or lose, you move on to another table and repeat. In cases where the point is 4 or 10 and you don't like laying those heavy odds, I suggest sitting out that decision.

That's pretty much it, with one very important stipulation: if more than one point passes while you're waiting, move on to another table and start fresh.

The hardest thing about playing this strategy is, of course, summoning the extraordinary amount of discipline you will need to avoid staying at the table for longer than one bet. I'm sure that many readers will question the notion of leaving a table that just produced a win, and might crank out *ten more* consecutive wins. Isn't that opportunity being ignored?

For those readers, I offer this variation: If you win, follow up with odds betting with a small odds bet on the don't pass side. Your objective is to ride a streak of wins, but in attempting this, 1) be sure to regress to a lower bet level for your follow-ups, and 2) leave after your very first loss!

THE RANDOM RED

Back in Chapter 5, you learned of the *Any Seven Parlay.* This procedure, also known as the *Random Red,* was designed to capitalize upon longshot opportunities that routinely occur at the tables, and it earns a delicious 20–1 return.

In that chapter, I was making the point that 7 is the most likely of all numbers (at craps) to be rolled *consecutively,* and, that streaks of three, four or five 7s in a row are not all that unusual. In fact, I've seen streaks of *six* consecutive 7s on quite a few occasions. Would you mind if I fantasize for a moment and project how much I could have made from one of those streaks, if I could have anticipated that event, acted upon it, and was not constrained by table maximums?

For this projection, we shall assume that six consecutive 7s were rolled, and I used the first one as the betting trigger, parlaying everything at each step:

LEVEL	BET	WIN	PROFIT
1	$5	$25	$20
2	$25	$125	$120
3	$125	$625	$620
4	$625	$3125	$3120
5	$3125	$15,625	$15,620

FIGURE 25
The Big Red Parlay
(Carried to an Extreme)

This five-stage parlay would return $15,620 from a $5 bet, in about one minute, provided that the dealers could process the calculations as quickly as for conventional wagers. On that basis, you could lose 3000 bets before winning, and still show a profit! This is mere speculation, for the table maximum would prevent you from making that bet. But the circumstances for making such a wager exist in casinos every day.

Now that you have seen the extreme, let's take a look at the *Random Red* as it was designed for this manual. Your focus will be on the triple sevens, and the betting scheme will look similar to the first two lines of Figure 25. But we need to adjust the figures a little to help mitigate the downside.

Using any (come-out) 7 as your trigger, you're going to start out with a $5 bet on the *Big Red*. If that loses, well, you're out five bucks. If it wins, though, instead of parlaying the whole $25, tell the stickman you want to *press it to $20*. That will enable you to recoup your original bet after winning the first stage of the parlay.

If the first two stages are successful, you will clear a cool $100 from the *random red*.

As noted back in Chapter 5, the best time to activate this wagering series is when you're seeing a tendency for multiple 7s in the casino where you're playing. Played selectively, one can reap handsome rewards from this bet. Just be sure to stay on top of things, and don't miss your cue.

THE RANDOM SISTER

This is one of the favorites in my gallery of surgical strikes, because sister number patterns frequently follow a path that has no relationship with the table temperature. That is, sister numbers can be conspicuously absent from a hot table, or, show up in abundance at an ice-cold table. Because of this, I tend to feel a little safer following the sister number trend, as a surgical strike, than to follow the line bet direction.

In this context, the term *surgical strike* pertains to a betting technique that involves moving to a new table after each series, regardless of the result. But you must first chart the table to see which side (do or don't) would have last produced a win, with respect to the sister number to the point. Then, you imitate that would-be win with a live bet.

What do you do when you're cued to lay the 4 or 10? You could choose any of the four options shown on page 124, but as a personal preference, I usually lay the number from the 5–9 group that lies closest to the point number.

How long is a series? I recommend either a single bet, or a two-stage progression (e.g., $15–$25) as your total investment in any table when on the do side. On the don't side, you'll need to lay a minimum of $25 against the 6 or 8, or $31 for the 5 or 9. Here, I recommend flat bets for as long as you continue to win, but be sure to leave after your first loss. And when in the lay mode, leave the bet 'working' if the shooter makes the point with no decision against your bet. Doing so will enable you to cash in on a continuous string of come-out sevens, which will fall into your lap from time to time!

THE RANDOM
DOUBLE EVEN

This is the *surgical strike* version of the *double even,* which was introduced on page 126. The only difference is that you will seek only one [win or lose] decision from each table, then move on to the next table or casino.

The betting trigger is the same as noted before: a number from the 6 & 8 group, and a number from the 4 & 10 group, rolled during the same come-out. The order in which they were rolled doesn't matter, and the point, if it happens to be an even number, counts as the first of the two numbers you seek.

Once you see your cue, place the two from each group that have *not* appeared, and await the decision. If you win, take down your bets right away and leave. And if you lose your bets, leave. Don't give the table another chance to get you!

When your bets on the 4 or 10 reach the $25 level or above, you do know what to do, don't you? On this, all knowledgeable gamblers agree: you *buy* the number instead of placing it. You do this because it's a major no-brainer, being a betting option that carries a considerably lower house edge.

Should you increase your bet size after each loss? That is a tricky question, because there are times when I think it's okay to do that, and other times when it isn't. Mainly, I think you should avoid the habit of increasing after every loss, but move to a higher betting tier after, say three consecutive losses. This will help mitigate the downside, should you happen upon a day when you hit a bad streak. Most of the time, however, I think you will be pleased with the results you get.

THE RANDOM FIVE EIGHT

The *Random Five Eight* is the product of an observation I made while reviewing some online wagering results. It appeared that the numbers 5 and 8 had a special relationship, in that one frequently followed the other.

Until then, I had been using the appearance of a number as its own wagering trigger. But after making the 5-8 observation, I realized I was targeting numbers that, having just been rolled, were statistically the farthest away from another appearance. In hoping to nab a cluster, I disregarded the overriding probabilities. This discovery is the basis for the *random five eight*.

What makes this procedure work? My feeling is that the passage of unrelated numbers pushes the expectation of an event to a place where it is statistically more "due." But this approach must not be confused with the pursuit of negative trends, where you target numbers after seeing huge gaps between those events. In those cases, you're 'fighting the trend.' Here, you are targeting the *neutral* table patterns (as noted back on page 29), which are the most common event sequences!

How is this procedure structured? When you observe this pattern: where the number 8 follows a roll of the 5, for example, wait for a new come-out to begin. Then, launch a two-stage place bet progression on the 8 after the *next* appearance of a 5, or a progression on the 5 after an appearance of an 8.

Note: if you lose the first stage of the progression, launch the second stage after the next point is established.

If that wins, the series is complete and you move on. If you lose the progression, repeat the process at a new table.

THE RANDOM SIX NINE

The *random six nine* is like the *random five eight,* except that your targets are the 6 and the 9.

Shortly after making the *five eight* observation, I studied more table results to see if the other two inside numbers also had a symbiotic relationship. It appeared to be so.

For this, the same rules apply, except that the 6 and 9 are substituted for the 5 and 8. But it should be noted that I advocate playing both strategies, depending on which one shows up first (after the triggers for both the 5-8 and 6-9 have been witnessed), rather than concentrate exclusively on one or the other.

Why? To help guard against the possibility that you might have hit a casino-wide trend where one of these two occurrences is sending out false signals. Since gaming trends can be very pervasive, pursuing a one-dimensional strategy could lead you into a trap. With a two-pronged approach, you're hedging against the possibility that one or the other of these two procedures is 'off-line' for the moment.

To clarify how to use these strategies in tandem:

After witnessing one example of the 5-8 connection and one of the 6-9, use the next appearance of one of those four numbers as the trigger to launch a progression on its counterpart. It matters not which number comes up first (even in the middle of a series), or if your wagering trigger happens to be the point. Just look at each pair as being inextricably linked.

If that bet loses, go to a new table and repeat the procedure, but be sure to start back at the beginning, where you await the betting triggers for each of the two pairs.

MIXED MEDIA

Mixed Media is the name I give to any group of procedures that function as part of a larger betting scheme. Technically, the merging of the *five eight* and *six nine* procedures, as suggested on the previous page, is a *mixed media* strategy. But it needn't be confined to two procedures; it can be a blend of any number of procedures that are logistically compatible.

For example, before heading out to the casino, you could designate the last four procedures shown in this chapter as your betting scheme for the day:

1) *The Random Sister,*
2) *The Random Double Even,*
3) *The Random Five Eight,* and
4) *The Random Six Nine.*

In doing so, you will alternate to the next procedure when losing. This is a must, because it helps you avoid getting caught in the net of some virulent casino-wide trend. Alternating after winning, however, is optional.

To implement the *mixed media* group shown above (if you choose that order), you would begin by determining the fate of a bet on the sister (to the point) at a table. If that (theoretical) bet would have lost, you lay the sister number of the next point. If your (live) bet loses, go to a new table and wait for your cue for the random double even. And if that loses, go to another table and play the five eight at the prompt.

The point of moving around is to dodge the insidious trends of gaming. Most of the time, it works!

THE SIGNATURE BET

A real man makes his own luck.
—Billy Zane, from the
1997 movie, *Titanic*

A *signature bet* is like a pet bet, which is played randomly yet regularly. Ideally, the performance of this wager should be tracked (with the *basic scorecard,* coming up), because in my experience, groups of random wagering results usually start to concur with the probabilities after thirty or forty trials. So, if my records show that these bets are overperforming, I prepare for the inevitable compensatory losing streak. If they seem to be under-performing, I prepare to harvest some wins. I have the edge, because I have an idea what to expect.

One example of a signature bet would be to bet a nickel on the yo (11) at the craps table whenever an 11 is rolled, expecting a double hit. Another would be to bet the hard 8, but only when 8 is the point. Yet another would be to bet on the big red whenever someone rolls a come-out seven.

The idea behind the signature bet is to choose a wagering situation that doesn't come up often, and is therefore something of a longshot. If you play it regularly and don't miss any betting opportunities, you will catch it often enough. Incorporating soft increases periodically is optional.

Chapter 12 contains a scorecard designed for keeping track of these wagers, which are actually auxiliary bets.

Whatever you choose for your signature bet, make it wild; make it interesting; make it fun!

THE SELECTIVE SHOOTER

And the earth becomes my throne
I adapt to the unknown
Under wandering stars I've grown
By myself but not alone.

—Metallica, from
Wherever I May Roam

Along S.R. 160, about 20 miles southwest of Las Vegas, a man with a scraggly beard was going about his morning routine. He put on a pair of jeans and a plaid shirt, and after finishing his coffee, doused the fire and rolled up his sleeping bag. Then he put his few possessions in a hiding place under a shelf-like rock, and headed for the road with his thumb out.

It was five minutes before the first car came by, a late model Buick that whizzed coldly past. Definitely not his ride. Shortly after that, however, a blue pickup came by, slowed down and stopped. Without a word, Lars opened the door, got in, and the truck sped off towards the city.

He told the driver he was going to the Flamingo Hilton, which was near the driver's destination. All he had was $32 in his pocket. He got out of the pickup in front of the casino and walked through the south entrance. After carefully choosing a place at a craps table, he laid twenty dollars on the felt, saying *"Three reds and five whites, please."*

He picked a spot to the left of the shooter, so he'd be next in line to shoot. When the dice came to him, he put a $5 chip on the pass line. He went on to make four points, then cashed out with a $64 profit, and left the casino.

Outside the casino he took in a breath of fresh air and stood there, looking around. Slowly and deliberately, he made his way to the Barbary Coast, next door. He bought in at another craps table, and like before, waited until the dice came to him before placing a bet. It took him just two minutes to wrangle a $38 profit, putting him $102 ahead for the day.

He then went to Tony Romas on Sahara Avenue for a meal of baby back ribs, then bought a pair of jeans and a carton of cigarettes before taking a cab back to his desert home.

After paying the fare, he had $32 in his pocket.

The *selective shooter* is a procedure for craps that involves backing only *yourself* at the tables.

Your objective is to get the dice as quickly as possible (at any given table), and bet your own roll only. Whether you pick a table with no players, or squeeze in at an active table to the left of the shooter (so that you'll be next in line to get the dice), it matters not. What's important is that you customize your play to the results you expect to get in that situation. For example, some players feel that inactive tables tend to produce more seven-outs than the ones where they squeeze in, so they might want to cater their betting toward that expectation, if they happen to choose an open (inactive) table.

My feeling on this is that anything that improves your win rate, can't be a bad thing to do.

In playing the *SS,* there's one question that will be foremost in your thoughts: *"Is this a pass or don't pass day?"* Generally, I find it easier to answer *that* question than to try to gauge the table temperature at any table at random. The reason for this, strange as it may sound, is that my abilities as a shooter frequently coincide with my moods. If I'm feeling confident and optimistic, it's a for-sure that I'll roll more numbers than when I'm upset. You may not understand how moods can affect table results, and I don't either. But if your income should depend on maintaining your success rate, you tend to accept, rather than question, your good fortune.

To me, the *SS* is the last refuge for those who need to win and have nowhere else to turn. If I was in a must-win situation (like the homeless man who was described), the *SS* is something I would certainly consider.

But until you get a feel for what kind of day you're going to have, you need to start out with small bets. After you've racked up some results from your own shoots, you might be in position to project the day's strategy. Each direction (do or don't) has its advantages, so don't try to induce a win from one side or the other. Accept what the table chooses to give you. Go with the flow, wherever that may lead.

If it ends up being a *pass* day, you could make a good day's pay in just ten minutes if you can roll fifteen or more numbers while backing yourself. And if you feel down and out, you can profit from that as well; you might be able to cash in on a large gathering of seven-outs that you induced.

In order to find the ideal conditions for doing this, it may be necessary for you to plan your visits for those times when the table conditions favor the player, that is, many tables to choose from; tolerable table minimums, etc. Certain times of day are better suited for this, and sometimes even the weather can factor itself into the picture.

Although the *SS* usually works well for me, I must caution you against overconfidence in your betting direction. There have been times when I would start out making more passes than not, and then suddenly my game just bottoms out, and I can't make a point for the next ten line bets. If I had been betting *right* the whole time, I'd have been slaughtered. Fortunately, my mood changes when I start losing, and if I bet the back line to match that mood, I generally come out okay.

It takes more effort and legwork to play the *SS* than to sit there and play the game like everyone else, but I find that the rewards justify that effort. When winning at casino table games is the only way one has to put food on the table, he doesn't usually mind putting out a little extra effort—if that's what it takes to succeed, and to survive.

SUMMARY OF
SURGICAL STRIKES

Circle and pounce.

—the Author

This page and the one that follows are quite possibly the most important pages in this book. The heart and essence of my gaming philosophy lies on these two pages.

Many readers aren't going to find it easy to warm up to the concept of surgical strikes, but if you're sincerely interested in winning consistently in the casinos, this is the shortcut. This is what it takes to make it happen.

Back in Chapter 2, I talked about the weapons the casinos utilize to get your money. One of these is called *continuum,* the nonstop succession of betting opportunities. The casinos keep the games moving so fast, they overwhelm you. They want you to dive in, have fun, and lose, lose, lose, because you can't keep up with the fast pace of the action they offer.

This is how the casinos trap you. This is how they get your money, every time. This is how they win, win, win, and line their vaults so they can build more casinos.

If you play the games the way they're meant to be played, you're doomed. You're destined to lose, and then lose again, and again, until your money is gone, or, you wise up.

Are you going to submit to this inevitability, or take control and use their facilities to your advantage? You can do it if you practice the art of selective wagering.

Some of the most successful gamblers I know make a good living as horseplayers. But boy, do they work hard. They spend five hours a day evaluating the information in the racing form; they check the horses in the paddock, scrutinize their behavior during the post parade, and then make their play at the window. All they're seeking is a handful of betting opportunities each day, and they play only the races where they spot a bargain that is overlooked by the public. We're talking maybe two or three solid bets in the course of a day. Perhaps a few more on some days, but that is compensated by other days when their analyses show that there's not a single playable race, the whole day. In that case they have the discipline to stay home.

This is what it takes for them to win, but my feeling is, they are doing it the hard way. Casino games carry lower percentages, by and large, than those found at the track. You can accomplish what they're doing with less penalty. But in order to do this, you have to see the games in a whole new light.

To a pro, the games are vehicles for turning over money, and nothing more. The games exist solely as a source of income, and have no entertainment value whatsoever. If you want to win, this is the kind of thinking you have to adopt.

Some people I've talked with have a completely different outlook. They'll lay $75 on the don't pass, then cover the rest of the place numbers with $78 or $81 across for four hits and down. They're trying to smother the layout with bets. This is exactly what the casinos love to see.

As I've been saying all along, you've got to take some time to size up the table. Once you think you've got it pegged, send in a battalion of your best men. If you do your homework, you'll win the majority of these battles.

The name I give for this mentality is *circle and pounce.* Like a hawk flying high above the trees, you circle the landscape in search of prey. When you find it, you pounce.

Circle and pounce; circle and pounce. That's how you succeed as a player in the casinos.

Most days, this will keep you in the winner's circle.

11

TIMING AND TEMPERATURE

Returning now to the subject of inanimate object behavior, we shall take a look at *table temperature.*

Realistically, there is no such thing as a *hot* or *cold* table at craps or any other casino game. The tables are inanimate objects and the results thereupon are purely random. Therefore, every table decision is independent of all others.

While it is true that the dice have no memory, no capacity for cognitive thought and no sense of time or place, table results often follow a path that *appears to be* consistent or predictable. As convincing as it may be, though, an abnormal table trend is nothing more than a random occurrence.

Is it coincidence when eight shooters out of eight seven-out by the fourth roll, as you will find at some tables? Is that just an aberration? Yep. The dice do not react to any of the previous decisions, and the table itself exerts no influence upon those results. But we call it a *cold* table, because of the need we have to give a name to the phenomenon.

That's all. Tables are never *hot, cold, warm* or *choppy.* These descriptions apply strictly to the *trends* occurring at a given table, at a given point in time.

154

TABLE TYPES:
PRELIMINARY DESCRIPTION

My experience has allowed me to identify 5 different types of craps tables, which of course refers to the playing conditions at the tables and not the tables themselves:

1) *The hot table:* The most lucrative table known to man. The points pass, and many auxiliary numbers are rolled.

2) *The warm table:* Also very favorable for right bettors. The dice pass more often than not, and many auxiliary (place) numbers are rolled along the way.

3) *The repeat table:* At such table, patterns are repeated. Single numbers; groups of numbers; patterns in general. A good money-maker if you tune into it.

4) *The cold table:* At this type of table, the majority of shooters can't make a single point. Lucrative for those playing the back line.

5) *The choppy table:* The most unpredictable (and worst) table you will ever encounter, for there is no consistent pattern to exploit. Unfortunately, it is also the most common of all the table types.

THE HOT TABLE

What It Is: The *hot table* is the most sought-after table type of all. Five-figure incomes can easily be made in an hour from a hundred-dollar buy-in, if one bets aggressively with the shooter who "refuses to die." Except for the very end, all the 7s show up during his come-outs, so he continues to roll the dice, make points and help the other players at the table benefit handsomely.

How to Identify It: Four ways. First, it's from where all the yelling and cheering (in any casino) originates. Second, the table layout will be lit up like a Christmas tree with place and come bets. Third, look at the chip rack directly in front of the shooter. If you see stripes in his columns of chips, that means the chips are coming in so fast he hasn't time to organize them. Fourth, everyone's racks should be loaded with chips.

How to Exploit It: Finding an opening isn't likely to be easy. If you are lucky enough to squeeze in and you think the shooter will last a while longer, you might want to lay a $100 bill on the layout and ask the dealer for *"Ninety-six across, please."* But be prepared for the possibility that you'll lose every dime of it in a St. Louis second!

If you do start catching some wins, press up the winning numbers one at a time in ten dollar increments or so until you've won enough to cover your investment. Then you may wish to go for larger gains. Occasionally, tell the dealer *"Same bet"* for five or six hits, as a hedge against the possibility that the seven will take all your bets down on the next roll.

There are more efficient ways to exploit such a table, but this is a simplified strategy.

THE WARM TABLE

What It Is: The virtue in a *warm table* lies in the scarcity of times you'll hear: *"Seven-out, line away."* Most shooters at such a table hold the dice for several minutes, which is a long time in craps terms. How many points they make is not really the issue. This table type is best known for all the place numbers rolled on the way to a line bet decision.

How to Identify It: Most (if not all) players at the table are happy and enthusiastic, and the numbered boxes on the layout are loaded with place and come bets.

How to Exploit It: A conservative approach would be to toss the dealer a green and say *"$22 Inside."* This will cover the four inside numbers (5, 6, 8 & 9), which have a greater chance of being rolled than any number except the 7. Collectively, these four numbers give you eighteen (out of thirty-six) ways to win.

You might wish to take down your bets after getting three, four or five hits and then wait for the next come-out to resume your betting, or you could leave them up until the 7 comes along and makes the decision for you. Then, replace those bets at the new come-out.

If the 4 or 10 are coming up quite a lot, you may opt to take some of your profit and cover one of them or both. Just be careful. In my experience, having bets on all six place numbers is tempting fate in a wanton and reckless manner.

If you wish to play more aggressively, you can bet larger, or press up your bets as you win. Just don't forget about the 7 that's always waiting in the weeds.

THE REPEAT TABLE

What It Is: From time to time, you may encounter the *repeat table,* where table decisions fall into a repetitious pattern. The more attuned you are to the possibility of this occurrence, the greater the chance you will reap its reward.

How to Identify It: A *repeat table* manifests its magic in many ways. A pattern of two passes, two don'ts, two passes, two don'ts. Tables where field numbers are rolled in long strings, or a 7 is rolled at every come-out. Tables where the number 9 passes whenever it's the point. Shooter after shooter rolls three numbers and then sevens out. Cold tables; tables where numbers come in pairs, or tables where every shooter makes his first point. These are all *repeat tables.*

How to Exploit It: It would be helpful if you get into the habit of notating the decisions at every table. This will help you see what's really going on. When a table is producing repetitive patterns, you'll become aware of it faster if you've been tracking the results. As soon as you've spotted an ongoing trend, pick up on it and move in for the kill. But it's no *monkey see, monkey do.* Look at the big picture. Envision the big picture. Become an inseparable part of the big picture!

Let me remind you once again that to do all this, you need to make an effort to stay detached from all the hyperactivity. The action at the craps tables can smother you if you don't perform a reality check on yourself periodically.

In Chapter 12 you'll learn about *customized scorecards* for craps, which help you organize the incoming data from the table. These help make your task a lot more manageable.

THE COLD TABLE

What It Is: The most enduring *cold table* I ever witnessed was at the Showboat in Atlantic City. It started out as a warm table, but the trend changed. I was late in picking up on the new direction, but I made out just fine.

As cold tables go, this one was a plum. No one ever rolled a 7 at the come-outs, though there were some 11s. The dice circled the table once, and every shooter went down with a crash. Normally when that happens the players start to leave, but it was Friday night, and all the tables were packed. None of the players at that table wanted to leave for fear of being shut out, but no one wanted to play the back line, either. They were there to party it up or die. So the players kept losing and I kept winning. *This has to end sometime,* I thought.

The dice went around the table again, but no one could make a point. As the dice were on their third trip, some working-class hero busted the trend and hit a point. Having cashed in on over twenty consecutive wins, I colored out.

That's what you call a *cold table.*

How to Identify It: Usually, the tables with fewer players. The mood is subdued, the chip racks are barren, and there are not a lot of bets on the layout. Some of the players betting the back line is also a tipoff.

How to Exploit It: As long as you don't get burned by the 7s at the come-out, play don't pass and take odds. If it helps your game, expanding to a *two-number don't* might maximize your potential for gain. And if the 7s show up during the primary come-outs, you can revert to *odds betting.*

THE CHOPPY TABLE

What It Is: The worst table you'll ever encounter. Also the most common table type there is. It's your worst nightmare and your most dreaded daytrip rolled into one. Whatever you do, this table will do the opposite. Until a recognizable pattern emerges, there seems to be no chance for you to win.

The choppiness of course pertains to the line bet results. The pass line will win some, but you never know when to expect what. Most of the time, the dice won't pass, but betting the back line is not usually a magical trip to Eden.

How to Identify It: It's that cursed place where nobody wins, no one has any fun, and the players are not in what you would call a happy frame of mind.

How to Exploit It: Real hard. The hot tip is to keep your bets small until the table starts showing signs that it is heading in a certain direction. Or, find another table.

What makes this type hard to exploit is its uncanny ability to do the opposite of whatever bet you choose. It's real tough to convert that kind of energy into something positive.

SUMMARY OF TABLE TYPES

What you don't know **can** *hurt you.*

—ITT Tech Commercial

Success as a craps player requires an awareness of the table types *and* the ability to anticipate changes in the table patterns. When the sands are shifting, you must pay special attention to all the particulars of that new direction, so that you lose no time adjusting your sights.

The sooner you can identify the emerging trend, the sooner you'll reach your daily win goal.

Every game in the casino has built-in snares you can't control, so your best move is to specialize in the exploitation of the one thing *they* can't control:

Gaming trends.

Aberrations of chance.

Flukes and anomalies.

Unexplainable phenomena. . .

. . . occurring every minute in a casino. Sooner or later, the table will tip its hand, exposing a pattern that will hold up for the next fourteen decisions.

This is where you step in and take control, for the beast has fallen into slumber. Understand: there is not a moment to lose. He could wake up at any moment.

THE SIX SIGNS
OF AN IMMINENT 7

You are at a warm craps table playing pass line with odds, and you have a couple of place bets up. You're doing pretty well, but suddenly the stickman is tapped on the shoulder. . .and your blood begins to run cold.

"Danger! Danger!" In your mind, red lights are flashing, a siren is sounding and you hear the loudspeaker announcement: *"Attention, please: This is a red alert. The stickman has just been replaced at craps table number nine."*

There's not a second to lose. You pull up your odds bet while telling the dealer, *"Off on my place bets,"* then toss a nickel to the stickman, saying, *"$5 big red."*

The new stickman pushes the dice to the shooter, who wipes out on that roll.

The loss of your pass line wager was unavoidable, for that bet can't be removed, but you saved your odds and place bets, and even made a profit with your big red bet. And all this was possible only because of your recently acquired awareness of the *six signs of an imminent 7:*

1) *One or both dice accidentally go off the table.*
2) *A new stickman replaces the present one.*
3) *You see a seven anywhere on the dice, at any time.*
4) *Two craps numbers are rolled consecutively.*
5) *Your place bets have not had a hit for five rolls.*
6) *The game is delayed because of a dispute.*

Am I saying that the dice *react* to the above?

Of course not. But if you pretend that they *will* react every time one of those six occurs, you'll save money.

Maybe it's the fact that the 7 is so ubiquitous, any excuse to pull up bets is going to help. Or maybe it's something cosmic. I can't explain why doing this will save you money, but I'm sure that if you play enough craps, you will come to agree with me. At any rate, here's what I advise:

1) *One or both dice go off the table:* Call your (pass line odds or place) bets off for three rolls. I frequently see a seven during that period.

2) *A shift change for the stickman:* Call your bets off for two or three rolls. After that, you should be okay.

3) *You see a 7 on the dice:* It matters not where you saw it or for how long; call your bets *off* for two rolls.

4) *Two craps numbers (2, 3, 12) are rolled consecutively:* Two craps numbers tells me that the 7 is preparing to pounce. Place bets *off* for two rolls.

5) *Place bets haven't hit for five rolls:* If your place bets aren't hitting, take them down. Doing so will probably save you money. This rule is different from the others, because you react to the *lack of* an event.

6) *The game is delayed because of a dispute:* Any protracted delay will *cool down* the dice, but take special heed if bad vibes are circulating. Place bets *off* for three rolls.

I wish I could give you a scientific reason for doing these things, for telling you this doesn't help my credibility, especially in light of the fact that if these signs *aren't* bringing 7s, *they may be ignored.* But experience has taught me that it is generally a good idea to heed these signals.

You really don't need a reason. Like I say, if it saves you money, it can't be a bad thing to do.

And any rule that gets you to pull your bets up periodically will probably work in your favor.

DICE FIXING

I fix my dice so that the threes are in a V position. Thus, the dice do not show a seven on any side.

—Frank Scoblete, from page 24,
Beat the Craps Out of the Casinos

I never pick up the dice so that the numbers on top or the side facing me add up to a number I don't want.

—Lyle Stuart, from page 161,
Winning at Casino Gambling

When the dice hit the far wall of the table, all the fixing in the world won't help you, for they will just bounce around in an uncontrolled pattern.

—John Patrick, from page 35,
John Patrick's Craps

The three quotes above pretty much run the full spectrum of opinions on the subject of *dice fixing,* which means setting the dice in a fixed position prior to the roll. One guy favors an exact position, the next is concerned with only two sides, and the third tells us that fixing is a complete waste of time.

Who to believe? Surely, one of these three opinions is more correct than the others, but which?

Lately, I've noticed that dice fixing has become the vogue. Used to be, the *fixers* would get hassled by the boxmen, but the casinos are more tolerant these days. Now that the trend has been firmly implanted in the national soil, maybe they consider *resistance to be futile,* as they say in deep space.

Regarding the opinions expressed on the previous page, who can say if any one of those is superior? Certainly not me. My preference is Frank Scoblete's V positioning, for I believe that it helps my game when betting *right.* But no one can prove what *would* have happened if another position were chosen, for a dice roll cannot be finitely duplicated.

To help you decide, let me present a few facts.

In my experience, many shooters have a tendency to roll the sister number immediately after establishing the point. Prior to that, the stickman probably forwarded the dice to him with the point number facing up. Guess what number is on the bottom? The sister number.

In my experience, I can induce the seven, often within three rolls, *if* the table is cold to begin with. Of course, if I could do this at any table, I'd own half the continent. But the (theoretical) fact remains: my percentages (to induce a 7) improve when I fix the dice to form a 7 on top, *if I'm at a cold table.*

In my experience, the craps shooters who end up having the longest rolls almost always turn out to be dice fixers. When I'm at a warm table and I see the shooter fixing the dice, I tend to have more confidence in his staying power.

I doubt that men of science will ever prove or disprove a causative link between dice *positioning* and *result,* so your best bet is to do what feels right. A couple tips, though:

1) Make sure both dice hit the far wall. The boxman will insist on this, but more importantly, failure to do so (frequently) seems to bring on an immediate seven-out.

2) Try to avoid hitting any chips or a player's hand. If the dice take a bad or unplanned bounce, this also seems to prompt a 7, quite reliably. You'll see.

12

CUSTOMIZED SCORECARDS

Choice is nothing without knowledge.

—United Health Care of Ohio

Fact is, those who play professionally don't use scorecards like those you're about to see. But I'm going to try to convince you that you can't succeed without them!

If you don't mind going through *what they went through,* you can forget about the scorecards. The trouble is, it took them years of bitter strife and a truckload of money to get there. Wouldn't you rather take the shortcut?

Customized scorecards help you to see the big picture, and to evaluate your performance after the fact. Every sliver of data you acquire in this way brings you closer to your goal of becoming an accomplished veteran of the games.

Even if you specialize in *one-shots* and seldom participate in extended sit-down sessions, scorecards can help you sort out the statistics that accrue. When your wagering data is compared to the probabilities, you might be able to piece together a realistic projection of what the future will hold.

166

THE BASIC SCORECARD

Having observed that I was notating every dice result at his table, the boxman (with a chuckle) called me a *dice counter*. But my habit didn't bother him a bit.

At another casino, when asked about my scorecard, I tried to convince a dealer that numbers get 'used up' on a pair of dice, at which point the dice can no longer produce those numbers, as a way of explaining why I was 'counting.'

Most of the time, no one pays any attention to my practice of tracking the table decisions. So much the better.

Figure 26 on the next page shows a customized scorecard for craps. Think of it as an itinerary, for it helps you see where you're going and what you need to do.

The top section is for time and place particulars. In the space at the top left, write the CASINO and its location. Moving from left to right, the three rectangles are for the MONTH, DATE and YEAR. To the right of that fill in the TIME the session began and then cross out the AM or PM that *doesn't* apply. LEVEL pertains to where you parked. Fill this out as soon as you park, denoting the aisle number or parking level, if applicable. After a harrowing day, you'll be glad you did!

Just below that area, the groups of boxes are for keeping track of up to five signature bets on each scorecard. The smaller of the two boxes is to check that a bet was made; the larger is for showing the monetary amount of that bet.

SN stands for *Sister Number*. Check the box if the *sister* was rolled on the way to a line decision. PT is to be checked if the point was made. The space in the middle is for table results, and the boxes at the right are to denote gains and losses.

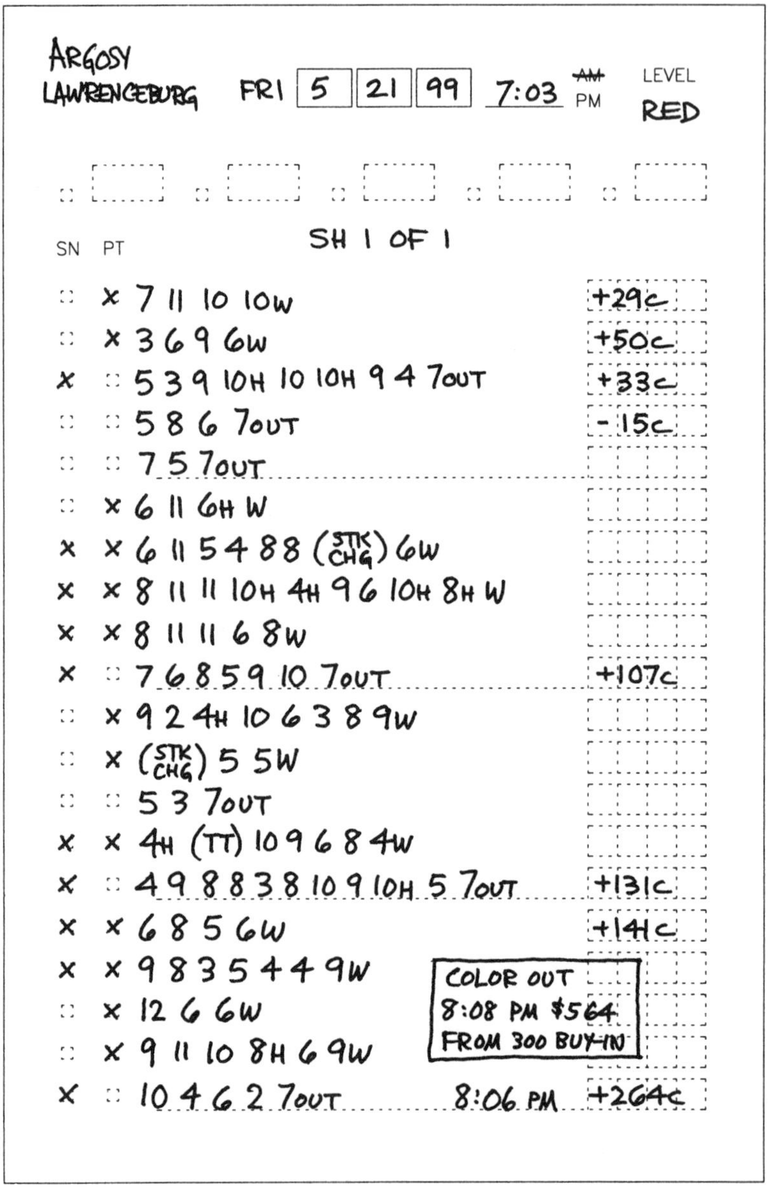

ARGOSY
LAWRENCEBURG   FRI 5 21 99 7:03 ~~AM~~ PM   LEVEL RED

SN PT   SH 1 OF 1

:: ✗ 7 11 10 10W   +29c
:: ✗ 3 6 9 6W   +50c
✗ :: 5 3 9 10H 10 10H 9 4 7OUT   +33c
:: :: 5 8 6 7OUT   -15c
:: :: 7 5 7OUT
:: ✗ 6 11 6H W
✗ ✗ 6 11 5 4 8 8 (STK/CHG) 6W
✗ ✗ 8 11 11 10H 4H 9 6 10H 8H W
✗ ✗ 8 11 11 6 8W
✗ :: 7 6 8 5 9 10 7OUT   +107c
:: ✗ 9 2 4H 10 6 3 8 9W
:: ✗ (STK/CHG) 5 5W
:: :: 5 3 7OUT
✗ ✗ 4H (TT) 10 9 6 8 4W
✗ :: 4 9 8 8 3 8 10 9 10H 5 7OUT   +131c
✗ ✗ 6 8 5 6W   +14c
✗ ✗ 9 8 3 5 4 4 9W   ┌─────────────────┐
:: ✗ 12 6 6W   │ COLOR OUT   │
:: ✗ 9 11 10 8H 6 9W   │ 8:08 PM $564   │
✗ :: 10 4 6 2 7OUT   │ FROM 300 BUY-IN │
                            └─────────────────┘
                            8:06 PM +264c

FIGURE 26
The Basic Scorecard

The *basic scorecard* has been designed to show all the relevant data that accumulates as you play. This version is the most efficient of all those I've tested through the years. It can help you spot betting opportunities and keep track of what stage you're at in your series or progression.

Figure 26 is a filled-in version of Figure 32 in the back of this book, which is intended to serve as a master for printing up your own scorecard pads. It is shown at full scale, which will result in a finished product that measures 4" x 6" when trimmed just inside the peripheral border. Have the printer bind them into pads of 50 sheets (apiece) for convenience.

This scorecard shows the table results from a live session at the Argosy riverboat casino in Lawrenceburg, Indiana. The scorecard shows the table decisions, and the natural ebb and flow of the money invested in the table.

During the Fig. 26 session, I had opted to show the flow of money in terms of cumulative gains and losses. That was denoted with a lower case 'c' after the monetary amount, as in +29c, seen on the first line of table results. Sometimes I prefer instead to show the plus and minus amounts that occurred on that line, and other times I add a 'W' or 'L' at the end to help me see how I'm doing at that table. That space is intended, however, to be used in whatever way best suits your needs.

In this example, I was playing at the $10 level, cautiously at first, but then betting larger as I started gaining confidence in the table direction. In some sessions I try to show the cumulative figures on every line, but I didn't in this case.

When certain events occur at the tables, I try to make note of them. For example, I use (DD) to denote *die down* (dice went off the table), and (TT) for *too tall* (dice landed on the armrest). Anywhere you see an 'H' after a number, that means it came up as a *hardway* number. And (Stk Chg) means a change in the shift rotation for the stickman.

Some readers aren't crazy about notating the table results, but I find that they are very helpful in organizing the data, and in evaluating my performance at the tables.

THE INTERNET
SCORECARD

To help you grasp the concept of the *Internet scorecard,* let me start out by saying that it actually does not exist. That is, in a form that's any different from the basic scorecard. But I make a distinction between the two because the format (the manner in which it is printed) is where the difference lies.

Figure 27 shows the layout of the Internet scorecard, as it should look on a letter size (8½ x 11) sheet of paper. Please note that this figure is shown at 50% scale.

To create this scorecard, you need to get two good copies of the basic scorecard as it appears in Figure 32 at the end of this book, then make a paste-up of the pair onto a sheet of paper, so that the end result looks something like Figure 27. Or you could have Figure 27 enlarged to 200%, but the resolution of that result may be poor. Ideally, you should get copies of Figure 32 and splice them into your enlarged copy of Figure 27. That way, the important features are sharp.

The reason for printing the Internet scorecard in this way is that at your home computer, you have more space to notate table results. In a casino, there is not room for a document this size. And just as important, it is less conspicuous.

Is it important to record Internet gaming results? Hell, yes! How else are you going to know if the table decisions are honest, and purely random? With documentation, you can compare the results you're getting against the probabilities, if you have doubt. As a backup, this is something that's nice to have.

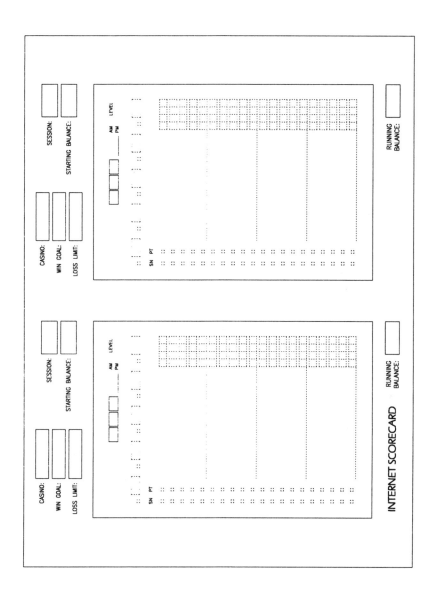

FIGURE 27
The Internet Scorecard
(Shown as a reduced paste-up)

THE STATISTICS SCORECARD

Finally, we come to the *statistics scorecard,* which is recommended for reviewing your performance at the end of the day, or, periodically. There are times when I like to know the scheme of things in terms of my overall win and loss ratios, and this is just the ticket for getting that information.

Figure 28 shows a completed statistics scorecard. The idea here is to review your primary scorecards and notate the wins and losses—on *this* scorecard—in the same order they occurred. This will help you keep tabs on that elusive big picture.

To illustrate, let's presume that you had been having rotten luck with your 2–1 bets, and had lost the last ten in a row. Well, if you play regularly, your deficit is accruing. If you continue to play, you're bound to hit a compensatory winning streak at some point, and you may be able to maximize that opportunity when it comes, if you're waiting for it. Now, don't be counting on the law of averages to set everything right before you bed down each night, but this data can provide valuable insights.

When I go on extended trips, I like to keep tabs on how I'm doing. If for some reason I'm getting caught in a snare in certain casinos, I want to know about it. Recognizing the problem is halfway to solving it, as they say at BP ProCare.

The small *W* to the left of the dashed columns stands for *Wins*, and *L* signifies *Losses.* Since 1–1 and 2–1 bets are staples for me, they have permanent places in the boxes at the left. The remaining boxes can be filled in to suit the need.

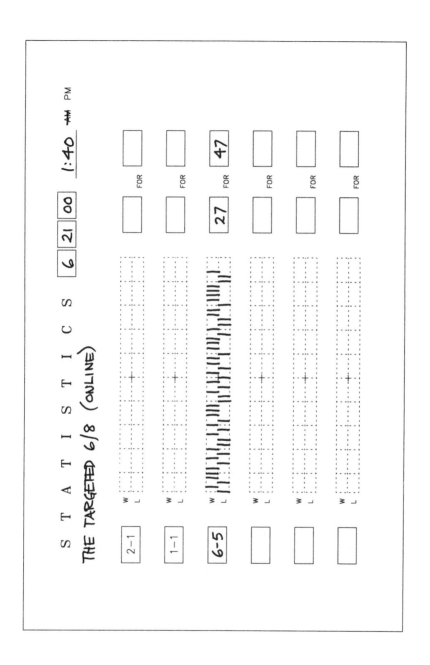

FIGURE 28
The Statistics Scorecard

SUMMARY OF
GAMING SCORECARDS

The position of this manual is that without scorecards to assist you, you are subjecting yourself to unnecessary hardships. With them, you can spot trends early, manage your money, and analyze your performance.

Two scorecards are designed for a finished size of 4" x 6", which is non-intrusive and inconspicuous, yet large enough to hold a generous amount of data. The other one, used for online wagering, is more suitable for playing at home.

To recap the scorecard types:

The *basic scorecard* gives you an overview of table trends, line bet direction and how you're doing monetarily. Unlike other players at the table, you have all the pertinent data about what the table *and you* are doing, at your fingertips.

The *Internet scorecard* gives you twice as much room for table data, because size and portability are of much less concern while sitting at your computer.

The *statistics scorecard* gives you a sense of perspective in terms of the collective betting activities. Are you holding your own or underperforming? This can offer insights into the history of your performance.

Together, these scorecards help you organize the table data. I like to think that Michael Douglas had it right, in the movie *Wall Street,* when he made the observation that *"Information is a valuable commodity."*

I couldn't have said it better.

13

THE PSYCHOLOGY OF PROFESSIONAL PLAY

This is the chapter that takes you into the mindset of those who specialize in table game play. How do they do what they do? How do they look at life? What are they like? What is it they know that gives them their edge?

SEEING THE BIG PICTURE

Sometimes you have to look back in order to move forward.

—From *Star Trek Voyager*

All of the successful table game specialists I've known have three things in common:

1) They are very focused on their specific goal.
2) No one else is doing what they're doing.
3) They are always attuned to the *big picture.*

What big picture? Where??

Seeing the big picture is part perception, and part attitude. It's how you see the *games* you play, the *numbers* they generate, and the *statistics* spawned from those numbers. Sometimes, the difference between success and failure lies in how one perceives that endless string of table decisions.

Most players have little or no regard for the big picture when they're in a casino. They stroll up to a table, make their buy-in and take their best shot. Their goal is to catch a hot streak; get lucky; make some easy money. They aren't looking for the big picture, and it never occurs to them to do so.

They don't see it. The casinos win.

Seeing the big picture means visualizing all your sessions as part of a connected chain. Information you acquired from yesterday's session can help you gauge the odds of the bet you're contemplating today. This, in fact, is the point of the *statistics scorecard,* of which you've just learned.

Seeing the big picture means not obsessing over the vigorish of a bet when table evidence overwhelmingly favors the occurrence. Occasionally, at racetracks *and* casinos, a 4–1 bet is surer than one paying even money. Are you gonna pass on a bargain like that? If you see a winner, go for it!

The trick, is to listen to what's in your head:

Hmmm, Haven't seen back-to-back 7s for a long time. Hmmm, the hardways aren't hitting today!

When things you normally expect don't occur on schedule, make a note of it. The stage is being set. The odds are changing. You can benefit from this.

In your daily routine, your objective is not much different from that of other professionals working in the field of finance. Just like them, you're turning over money, using your expertise to seek a profit as you do so. Your job is harder, because you're closer to the firing line, but just like them, you must always keep the big picture in your sights.

NICKEL MIDNIGHT

Like an athlete who can smell victory, he pays no heed to the punishment he absorbs.
　　　　　　　　　　　　　　—Margaret A. McGurk,
　　　　　　　　　　　　　　reviewing *Donnie Brasco*

There was not even six inches between me and the player to my right, but the young African American insisted on squeezing in. My neighbor didn't complain, so I overlooked it. The new player stood there fidgeting with a bunch of reds and greens in his hand. Then he spied my scorecard.

"Any 2s come up lately?"

Looking at my card, I responded, *"Yeah, there was one just three rolls back."*

"What about 12s? You seen any 12s come up in the last forty rolls?"

Again I checked the card and saw none since beginning the sheet, nearly forty rolls back. I told him so.

Immediately, he pulled a nickel from his hand and tossed it toward the stickman. *"Nickel midnight,"* he said.

His one-roller on the 12 did not win. He repeated the bet, again and again, taking no heed to his losses. Finally he won, eleven rolls into the bargain.

"One forty-five and down; move it to the two," he said. The stickman moved his nickel to the 2, and the dealer put $145 in chips on the layout in front of him.

Five rolls later he won another $145 on the 2.

"Move it to the 12?" asked the stickman. He nodded.

After losing the next twenty rolls—during which time two 2s came up (but no 12s)—he left the table. The tally was two wins and thirty-five losses against a longshot that paid 29–1, for a net gain of $115 in about 30 minutes. But had he quit after the second win, his profit would have been $215.

He fit the description noted on page 175: focused on his goal; doing something different; tuned to the big picture.

I had often considered going after the 2 or 12, but wasn't sure how to proceed. Seeing his betting scheme opened my eyes. The dude had put some thought into it, and made some choices. Then he had the guts to follow through on his plan.

Up to that time, what kept *me* away from chasing longshots like that was intimidation. I thought I'd be a nuisance with my bet requests every five or ten seconds. I thought I'd look like a fool when I kept losing and losing.

It's not like that at all. The stickman is there to help you. After that player had placed his second consecutive bet, the stickman was there with his hand out, waiting to catch the chip for the next one.

The bettor didn't have to say a word. The repeating bet was understood. And another thing: he didn't look like a fool when he got paid $145 for his $5 bet, twice!

Seeing the big picture means seeing beyond the rain. Putting trust in the fact that the oasis is out there. Visualizing victory in spite of the long odds.

Is this strategy viable? That's for you to decide. I don't play it, but I think it could work. If you try something like this, though, the most important things to consider are your win and loss limits. You can't go out there and bet upward to infinity, because some tables will not cooperate. If the dude had set a win goal of *two* wins, he'd have done much better, but doing so may have hurt him in a previous session.

Who can say?

Seeing the big picture means looking at the whole instead of the fragments. Use your imagination, be creative, and never forget that *eventually,* every dog has his day.

THE PROFESSIONAL'S OUTLOOK

To whatever extent possible, a seasoned player places his bets when the conditions for winning are ideal. But . . . how does one do that? How can one anticipate a table game decision with any degree of certainty?

If you've been paying attention, you should have some idea how it's done. For example:

After a shooter rolls three (or more) come-out sevens, the hot tip is to lay the point.

If everyone at the table is cheering and whooping it up, only an idiot would play the back line.

When you keep getting burned by craps rolls every single come-out, isn't it time to think about hedging?

If you're losing, losing, and losing, maybe it would be a good idea to take a break!

After conceiving the sister system, I tested it with live bets, and bombed out Big. Why? I forgot to confirm the *presence of that trend.* Before betting on that expectation, I should have waited until seeing at least one would-be win.

You wouldn't spend a whole morning fishing in a lake that wasn't stocked, would you? Well, don't set your sights on a target whose existence has not been confirmed.

Having the discipline to await the right table conditions is what separates the amateurs from the pros.

BATTLING BACK

Above all, challenge yourself. You may well be surprised at what strengths you have, what you can accomplish.

—Cecil M. Springer

If I was called upon to name one reason for my longevity in this field, it would most definitely be my talent for *battling back*. That is, my ability to salvage a losing session.

Very seldom do I hit a winning streak right off the bat, which means that most of the time, I start out in the hole. And when that happens, I pretty much forget about trying to win. All my thoughts are focused on *getting back to zero*.

Accomplishing this is never easy. You lose $200 in just fifteen minutes, and now you're going to have to spend the next hour and a half getting it back. When you accomplish that, *then* you can start thinking about looking for ways to win.

Perhaps it will work out differently for you, but as I see it, the only way you're going to have a chance to make it in this area is to specialize in battling back. Learn how to dig yourself out of a hole. Squeeze out a win against the odds. Defy Mother Nature, gravity, and all the laws of physics.

It's not easy, but it's doable. All you need do is remember the lesson from way back on page 7:

*Before you can learn to win, you must learn how to **not** lose.*

In this area of expertise, there is no greater truth.

A DAY IN THE LIFE

I read the news today, oh boy . . . about a lucky man who made the grade . . .

—John Lennon, from
A Day in the Life

I open my eyes and look to the left. The digital clock on the dresser says 9:06. I raise my head and turn to the right. Outside the window I see the boardwalk; beyond that the Atlantic Ocean. It's a beautiful fall day.

It's my eighth day in Atlantic City. From my bed, I grab a 3 x 5 index card and look at it:

			(CUMULATIVE)
MON	9–5	+140	+140
TUE	9–6	+442	+582
WED	9–7	+464	+1046
THU	9–8	+204	+1250
FRI	9–9	+514	+1764
SAT	9–10	+360	+2124
SUN	9–11	+190	+2314

Average Daily Win: $330

Today is the twelvth of September, the first day of my second week in Atlantic City. My first week's earnings reflect that I had a fairly good week. I'll go out again today, but not tomorrow, as I don't usually gamble on the thirteenth.

After cleaning up, I put on my jeans and one of my two-pocket shirts. The latter is a necessity: I use the pockets for scorecards, notes, pens, chewing gum, whatever. This keeps my hands free.

Every morning I go out and purchase my copy of *The Press* (Atlantic City's newspaper) from a machine. Doing so gives me a chance to get exercise and take in the boardwalk ambience. This morning, however, I had to go five blocks before coming to a machine that wasn't sold out.

At 10:00 I'm having a $3.95 breakfast in one of those dives right on the boardwalk. For a few bucks more, I could've had a fantastic meal at the Showboat or Resorts buffet, but a large meal before a session tends to dull one's edge.

Better to stay hungry.

10:30 am: I'm back in my hotel room, sitting on the bed and clipping out newspaper articles about casinos. My schedule for the day is pretty light, so I take my time reading the paper and thinking about the day's strategy.

11:15 am: I'm on my way out the door once again. I picked the Sands as my starting point for the day. Upon arrival, I see that only two craps tables are active, and there's no room at either one. I'm on my way out when I happen to notice someone walking away—which provides an opening.

"Change only," I say to the dealer as I lay three bills on the table, *"no action in the come."* I put the chips in my rack and note the casino, time and date on my scorecard, then I take a moment to check out the players.

"How's the table running?" I ask the gentleman to my left, an older man with thick white hair. He had about $60 in his tray and a $5 pass line bet with double odds.

He glances at me and grunts, *"Cold."*

"Seven-out, line away, 8 was," says the stickman as the dealers scoop up the losing bets.

After watching another line decision, I decide on my strategy for that table: the *sister system* for my primary bets and the *two-number don't* for my secondaries.

After about thirty minutes, I left the table and collected my $120 profit at the cashier window. Then I took a seat at one of the console slot machines next to the cashier and finished filling out my scorecard.

I glance at my watch as I attempt to get past the *waddlers* (obese, middle-aged ladies who exist solely to obstruct casino foot traffic) near the front entrance, and finally break free. It is ten minutes past noon.

Outside, I cross the street and enter the Claridge. I get a drink of water and then check out the gaming area.

Immediately my attention is drawn to a craps table in the center of the room, where the players are excited. To someone like myself, it sounded like an opportunity.

To my delight, I learn that the point is 4. There's no time to lose. I peel a bill from the wad of money in my hip pocket, then pull a five from my wallet. Squeezing in, I wait for the right moment, lay $105 on the table and say *"Buy the point for $100."* The dealer converts my money to four greens (which he puts inside the *"4"* box) and one red for the commission. Then the boxman passes a *buy* button to the dealer, who sets it atop the stack of greens.

Within ninety seconds the shooter makes the point, and my $100 buy bet wins $200. *"Take down my buy,"* I tell the dealer, and he pushes twelve greens in front of me. As I start to head for the cashier, I notice that the boxman (who for some reason was wearing a college varsity sweater) is watching me like a hawk. Very odd. They don't usually pay much attention to me on those occasions that I make a random buy.

After getting my money from the cashier, I take a seat at a slot machine on the south wall and update my daily earnings record: $315 profit, and it's 12:21 pm. It is just a little more than an hour from the time my workday began.

Outside, I continue my southward trek and head for Bally's Park Place, just across the street. After giving a buck to one of the panhandlers, I enter through the side door and take the escalator up to the casino.

Three craps tables are open: a $5 and a $10 table that are filled with players, and a $25 table where the crew waits for a customer. There's no room at the two active tables, and I'm not in the mood to warm up the high-minimum table.

I leave through the boardwalk entrance and make my way to Caesars. It's unseasonably hot for September. The beach is packed with sun worshippers. Seagulls and terns squawk noisily overhead as I weave through all the vacationers. Not a moment too soon I arrive at the air-conditioned comfort of Caesars. I go through the first set of doors, past the guard and then through the second doorway.

I need a drink of water. That's one thing you should know about all the moving about you're likely to do: sometimes you're never in one place long enough to cop a free drink. Not that they were ever free for me anyway. I never let my server leave with less than a dollar gaming token for a tip.

It's 1:37 pm, and I have just made another $114 playing the sister system at a table (at Caesars) that was fairly cooperative. I'm now $429 ahead and done (working) for the day. I head up to the Ocean One Pier, right across the boardwalk from Caesars, and make a beeline for a place called Gourmet Burger, where I get a cheeseburger platter with extra cheddar. After finishing that, I go to the French bakery on the other side of the food court and get a palm cake for dessert.

My original plan was to go to Trump Plaza after Caesars, but since I had reached my daily win goal, I decide instead to rent a rolling chair to take me back to my hotel.

After taking a nap and watching some TV, I meet a friend in Brigantine, and later we have dinner at the Showboat.

Not a bad day. Not a bad life.

14

ONLINE WAGERING

Online wagering. Internet gambling. Cybercasino gaming. These phrases, which didn't exist just a few years ago, are now common language for describing a multi-billion dollar business: placing live bets from your home computer.

If you have ever considered gambling on the Internet, some rather troubling questions may have given you pause:

1) Is Internet gambling legal?
2) Can the operators of those sites be trusted?
3) Are the games honest?

These are not frivolous issues: the possibility of doing prison time; or that your charge card could be subject to massive unauthorized charges; or that someone might be *right there* to push a button whenever you bet large.

But a substantial number of people do it every day, right? Doesn't the *safety in numbers* rule apply here?

Yes, no, or maybe. As you read this, the rules are changing at state and federal levels. And the wheels of big government are inclined to turn very slowly whenever they take on a tough, complicated issue like this one.

185

THE LEGAL ASPECTS

Before contemplating the question of whether you'd like to try online wagering, it would be a good idea to know something about *the legal aspects*. Meaning, the risk to *you*. Now, we all know that risk is inherent in all forms of gambling, but we like to think that the risk is controlled. We don't need to compound it with the possibility of civil penalties, or financial debts that we did not incur.

To help you get a handle on this matter, you should know some of the history of what the government is trying to do, and why this issue is so difficult to resolve.

Back in 1995, Senator Jon Kyl from Arizona introduced an amendment to the Crime Prevention Act of 1995, known as the Internet Gambling Prohibition Act. It was passed by the U.S. Senate, but didn't make it through the House of Representatives. In the years that followed, it was reintroduced with significant amendments, but none of the versions have succeeded in passing both houses of Congress, as of the date of this writing.

The original bill contained a provision making it a federal misdemeanor to place a bet over the Internet, but that effort has since been abandoned. However, the state of California is trying to pass a tough anti-Internet gaming bill, which would make the bettor at an online gaming site subject to a fine of up to $100 per transaction. So, readers, be advised that state laws might end up superseding those of the federal government.

Why is it so difficult for Congress to pass a law to restrict Internet gaming? There are some pretty good reasons.

Chiefly among them is the question: how can the U.S. or any state government impose its authority on a transaction that originates from outside its borders, without impinging on the sovereignty of a foreign government? Virtually all online casinos are based outside the U.S., in places like the Caribbean, Europe, and Australia. Some governments operate the games themselves! Liechtenstein will accept bets from anywhere in the world, with the exception of its two relatively powerful neighbors, Austria and Switzerland. So what it comes down to is this: since websites are passive and the user receives the signal electronically, there is no way to stop it at the border. Also, international law does not allow for one country to arrest a citizen of another country, who may in fact be licensed by his own government.

Compounding the problem is this: even if the PC could be eliminated, a website called MonaCall offers cybercasino gaming from a touch-tone phone!

What about the Internet service providers? Can't America Online, for instance, be held accountable? Under current law, the telephone companies and the Internet access providers are not criminally liable if, say, an illegal bookie uses a telephone line. Moreover, there would be enormous public outcry if the utility companies began monitoring the habits of all their customers. However, the state of Nevada has passed a bill that makes it a state crime to "knowingly" transmit a wager to or from Nevada, via the Internet. But this is hard to enforce.

What's left? Prosecuting the bettors? Well, the U.S. Department of Justice doesn't want to be in the business of arresting gamblers. To shut down the market, they'd have to criminalize a whole new segment of the population.

But that doesn't stop individual states from making their own laws, however flawed they may be. As of June, 2000, quite a few of the fifty states have either passed laws or have legislation pending that make accepting a wager over the Internet a crime. The penalties are not severe, but if you are attracted to the notion of Internet gambling, it is the recommendation of this book that you check out the laws within your state.

ASSESSING THE DOMAIN

As of June, 2000, there were 847 online casinos operating on the Internet, according to *BettorsReview.com,* a website that ascribes ratings to virtual casinos, based on their own studies and on consumer feedback. Out of those, 336 were on their Blacklist, which is a list of all the online casinos that have had problems at some point in the past. These include payout problems, company problems, not having a license to operate, or a lack of adequate customer support. It is suggested that you peruse this list before placing bets with an online casino.

But that still leaves over 500 sites from which to choose. How does one narrow it down?

BettorsReview also has a listing of top sites, as determined by the public. But my personal preference for making that choice is to check out rgtgaming.com, an online gaming magazine that is hosted by Frank Scoblete. I feel that this site is the best source for gaming-related news, stories, tips and associated information. And I tend to have more confidence in the online casinos that are advertised there, because, as I understand it, they do not allow their site to be a platform for advertising by online casinos that have anything less than the best reputation.

I therefore recommend that you visit these two websites to help guide you toward a suitable online casino.

Once you have made a choice, however, how do you assess the domain? How do you determine that it's honest, and that the gaming results they offer are random? This is no small matter, for quite a bit of your money may be at stake.

To help you get an idea about who or what you're dealing with, here are some things you should know:

1) Almost all online casinos use random number generators to create their gaming results, which are part of the program sold to them by the software manufacturer. Most of these programs are encrypted by the software company, locking out the casino's ability to modify the programming.

2) These software programs record all the bets and results, and the time they occurred. Everything you did while wagering online can be reconstructed.

3) Most online casinos don't get your credit card number. The monetary transfer is handled by a third-party processor, who forwards the money to the casino.

4) In an effort to overcome public distrust of online betting, and in the absence of global regulation, the industry is trying to regulate itself. If a casino is a member of the Interactive Gaming Council, the Internet Gaming Commission, the Antigua-Barbuda Directorate of Offshore Licensing, or the Ethical Online Gaming Association, it should be okay. You'll know they're a member if you see the official seal of one of the above, at the site.

5) If the casino has good phone or email support, this tends to indicate that it's a reputable casino.

6) Some e-casinos and many of the software developers are publicly-traded companies, which means that their books are open to the world. And they wouldn't stay in business for very long if they engaged in unethical business practices.

Then there's something else to consider: at a larger site, do you think the casino has the manpower to monitor all the games in progress at any given point in time? We're talking about a company hiring thousands of people to sit there and doctor up the table results, and keep it a secret from the rest of the world, forever? I don't think so. They couldn't meet the payroll. And why would they bother, when the games are already constructed to grind out a steady profit?

But what are the chances that a program could respond to betting increases, or "kick in" when a player is ahead?

One of the nagging concerns of any potential player at an Internet casino is the fact that you're playing with invisible dice. Although you see animated graphics that look like dice rolling on a table, you know that it's not real. It's just a computer program. That being the case, what's the chance that someone might have access to a 'magic button' that can cause your bet to lose when you've hit the last stage of your progression?

Such is a player's worst nightmare. And unless you run the casino, there's no way to know for sure.

One of the very first cybercasinos, established in 1995, uses the Internet to access an independent random number generator that produces its gaming results. And to ensure compliance with Las Vegas standards, the payout percentage is certified on an ongoing basis by PriceWaterhouseCoopers.

This is of some comfort, but many gambling sessions come down to a just few key bets. Modifying a few results won't skew the percentages noticeably. So, what's to prevent an enterprising individual from doctoring certain results?

As noted on the previous page, most of the software used by online casinos have programs that can't be altered. But I must confess to having doubts of my own.

What I suggest is to start out betting small, and notate all of the table decisions. After 5000 dice rolls, you can do a study of those numbers and see if they concur with the probabilities. If something is truly out of whack, it'll show up. And then you'll have documentation to support your case.

But the key question is: *are you winning?* If you are, this is a good sign. Keep betting small until your bankroll grows to where it can support larger bets.

One final criterion for assessing the domain: If you're going to play per the advice of this book, be sure to pick a casino that has what are called *multi-player games,* or the equivalent. What you don't want is a cybercasino that obligates you to have a bet riding with every single roll of the dice. The multi-player games let you see "how the table's running" before placing a bet, and to me, that's worth a lot.

TRACKING YOUR BETS

As added insurance against the possibility that table game results aren't legitimate at an Internet casino, it is recommended that you notate all the table decisions as you play. The *Internet scorecard,* which was discussed in Chapter 12, is ideal for this. And, if properly used, it will also show the monetary flow of the wagering activity.

So, how does one authenticate a group of random wagering results? Let's say that you want to check the statistics of the 5 or the 9 at an online craps table where you recorded the results, and your sampling is at least two thousand dice rolls. For either of those two numbers, the true probability is 2:3. This means that if you are (place) betting one of those numbers continuously, you should win two out of every five bets, on average. Consequently, along the way to getting your two thousand dice rolls, you might see the numbers match the probabilities, perfectly, several times. If not, you may have a problem.

The probabilities for the 4 or 10 are 1:2, which means that a bet on either number should win one out of every three attempts. The 6 and 8 are harder to calculate, because the 5:6 true odds means that a place bet on either number should win five times out of eleven. And as for the number 7: that should come up once out of every six numbers rolled.

But there is another, larger purpose for tracking your bets. You need to see the history of your performance, so you can see if you've been sticking to your game plan. To put it plainly, it helps keep you honest: *with yourself.*

ONLINE STRATEGIES

Do you think that you could be content to seek out just a handful of betting opportunities a day, if you knew those wagers were highly targeted, precision bets?

Online wagering, as luck would have it, is perfectly suited for the style of play advocated in this book, particularly with regard to *surgical strikes.* Tell you why:

When you walk into a for-real casino, you're on *their* turf. You're in an environment that was specifically designed to make you lose control and feel good about it. You're inundated by the sights and sounds they created to trigger your compulsive nature. You are putty in the hands of the master craftsman.

Now, maybe you're the one who can rise above all of that, but the casinos don't make it easy. Standing at a craps table for long periods, waiting for a certain table condition so you can place a single bet is not a walk in the park. In the midst of all the activity at the table, you tend to feel awkward and conspicuous. All eyes are upon you. You gonna bet, or what?

Not a problem when wagering online.

Then there's the time spent traveling to the casino, money for gas, and sometimes, admission. It adds up.

Of course, if you're looking for fun, then go to the casino. Go and lose, like all the others. My words are directed to those who want to profit from their wagering activities.

Betting *selectively,* while seated comfortably at your desk, makes the process a whole lot easier. By the end of this chapter, I hope you come to see the truth in that.

THE TARGETED 6-8

The first time I tried out this strategy, I won twenty-one out of my first twenty-three sessions. You won't always do that well, but I'm convinced that this technique holds more promise than most strategies I've seen, and it's much easier to do online than in a 'real' casino.

The *targeted 6-8* is a spinoff of the *mixed media* combination of the *random 5-8* and the *random 6-9,* but it's more precise. What you're looking for is a 'would-be win' from each of those two categories, then after the next come-out, you can begin your search for the appropriate wagering target.

You're seeking an example where a roll of a 5 would act as a successful betting trigger for a place bet on the 8, or vice versa. Please note: it matters not which triggers which. But you're also looking for a similar situation with the 6 and 9. Again, it doesn't matter which came first, the 6 or 9, or which group (5-8 or 6-9) came up first. All you're waiting for is to observe a successful linking of the 6 & 9 and the 5 & 8. Once you reach that point, two more things have to happen:

1) you must wait until a new come-out begins, then:

2) you must wait until a 5 or a 9 is rolled.

After fulfilling those two requirements, launch a two-stage wagering series on either the 8 (if a 5 was spotted first), or the 6 (if a 9 came up). Once you start your series, play it through to the bitter end. Meaning, if you lose the first stage of your series, replace the number (at a higher level) immediately after the next point is established.

What makes this strategy different from the mixed media combination of the random 5-8 and 6-9, is that it's a one-way deal. To increase the win rate, bets on the 5 or 9 (that would have been triggered by an appearance of an 8 or 6), are not included in the procedure. That way, you're targeting only the 6 or the 8, and only one of them at a time.

How should the two-stage progression be configured? For starting out, I would recommend a $6 bet at the first stage and a $12 bet at the second. If you lose both bets, write off the loss as irretrievable and resume, next time, at the same level. After you get the hang of it, you may want to go to a higher wagering tier after losing a series (to recoup losses more quickly), but I don't recommend doing that until you've mastered the basic procedure, and have an idea what win rate to expect.

Keep in mind, random gaming results might vary from one online casino to the next. I honestly don't know if they do or not, but I'd advise against making assumptions.

Figure 29 shows a scorecard where the win came at the second stage of the series. (But just so you know, most of my wins come at the first stage.) The row of handwritten numbers at the far right indicate the number of dice rolls up to that point, which I note for my own reference. As this figure shows, it took over fifty rolls for me to nab the win. Most times, it takes around thirty rolls or more, but I've done it in fifteen.

Note that the trigger for the 5-8 occurred on the second line. There, the 8 would have been a successful trigger for a place bet on the 5. Remember, when establishing the trigger, it matters not which order the numbers showed up. All you need is to spot a positive link between the two.

As for the 6-9 trigger, that didn't come until the tenth line, which ended at roll number forty-four. But you still have to wait for the next come-out to commence, and then wait for a 5 or 9 to appear. That happens on line 12, but leads you straight into an ambush. Don't sweat it. It happens. As you can see, when you re-placed the 6 at a higher level after the next come-out, you caught your win on the fourth roll.

(ONLINE)

FRI | 6 | 16 | 00 | 9:02 ~~AM~~ PM   LEVEL

SN	PT					
	x	7 6 5 6H W				4
x	x	6 8 5 5 6W				9
x		2 9 4 5 10H 7OUT				15
		8 7OUT				17
		10 11 7OUT				20
		7 5 7OUT				23
	x	8 8W				25
x		7 7 7 9 8 8 5 7OUT				33
	x	11 12 3 6 6W				38
x	x	9 6H 10 12 5 9W				44
	x	4H 4W				46
		9 4 7OUT	-6			49
x		9 10 5 6H 4 4 4 7OUT	+14			57

RESULT: +8
BALANCE: $722

FIGURE 29
The Targeted 6-8 Scorecard Results

Some readers who are unfamiliar with the game might have difficulty understanding what constitutes a "betting trigger" and what makes up a "would-be win." In this application, a *trigger* is simply an appearance of a number that is sought. This can occur at any moment a game is in progress. A *would-be win,* however, cannot include the establishment of the point. The reason for this is that place bets are normally "off" or "not working" during the come-out, as protection from come-out sevens.

Also, a *would-be win* does not have to occur during the same come-out as the *betting trigger.* All that matters is that the trigger would have served as a cue to proceed with a (successful) bet on the appropriate wagering target.

The hardest thing about playing this procedure is that after getting your single win or losing the series, you must stop. Don't try to squeeze out more wins. Exit the program, then start over at a later time. This is the best way.

ADDITIONAL ONLINE STRATEGIES

Anything you can do in a "real" casino can be synthesized online, with the exception of non-wagering activities like the $3.95 steak dinners or visits to the spa. Therefore, you don't need me to tell you how to do this or that online. Just follow the rules as you would in a normal gaming environment.

There is one thing I would suggest you change, however, in your approach to beating the games. When betting online, start out slow. Don't try to hammer your way to victory. This advice, of course, makes sense in all gaming situations, but I think that it is especially important to exercise caution online.

When the dice are technically a cartoon, you never know exactly who or what you're dealing with!

THE PROS AND CONS OF ONLINE WAGERING

What's good about online wagering? What's bad about it? Here's the picture, as seen from my vantage point.

The pros:

1) Travel expenditures to and from casinos are eliminated. This includes, gas, maintenance, and if you lease your vehicle, mileage penalties.
2) It's more convenient. No longer must you spend hours of your time in transit.
3) Admission is always free.
4) Most online casinos offer matchplay bonuses of 10% or 20% of your buy-in amount. Free money!
5) There is no pressure to place a bet. You can wait all day for the right table condition, if you want.
6) You are detached from all the sensations casinos use to try to bring out your compulsive side.
7) Since they have lower overhead, e-casinos can give you better payouts for some bets. *Intercasino,* for example, pays 4:5 for laying the 6 or the 8, *without* the usual $1 house commission attached. Also, many virtual casinos pay better for certain proposition bets.
8) Playing while seated comfortably at a desk in your own home is just flat-out more comfortable!
9) Many virtual casinos have (free) practice modes. Some sites in fact offer nothing *but* practice games.

And now, the cons:

1) The accessibility of online casinos (one of the pros), can instead be a liability for those who can't handle the seductiveness of gaming. *Click a mouse, lose the house* is not widely regarded as a happy thought.

2) Use of a credit card (frequently used for the buy-in) tends to keep a player detached from the realization of the ultimate cost. This can easily compound the damage noted in item 1.

3) In trying to nab the matchplay bonus (which requires a stated minimum amount of play), some players stay at the tables longer than intended, causing them to lose more than intended.

4) Some online casinos are downright dishonest. They are a vanishing breed, but you can't assume that all casinos are legit. Choose your site carefully.

5) Online gambling may be illegal in your state. Although the penalties are not severe, you should investigate the matter before getting in too deep.

6) For those who like the sights and sounds associated with real casino gambling, as well as the free drinks and bargain meals, it ain't the same.

You may have noticed that there are fewer *cons* than *pros*. Don't be fooled. The negatives may be fewer in number, but they carry more weight, because we're talking about the possibility that people's lives may be ruined.

Some people may take comfort in knowing that large credit card debts to online casinos, when challenged by the person who racked up the bills, are frequently uncollectable. Meaning, the bank or credit card processor will side with the gambler (its customer) over what is oft presumed to be some kind of sleazy offshore operation. But relying on this as a bail-out procedure is a really *bad* idea!

The best advice: Be careful.

SUMMARY OF
ONLINE WAGERING

So, what's the verdict? Is the availability of online wagering a blessing, or a curse?

As with most things, it's what you make it to be. Some will misunderstand the concept, and think they've found a path to easy money, only to make a shocking discovery later on. Others will see it as an opportunity to play games of risk without all the time and expense that would otherwise accompany a trip to a casino that has real gamblers, casino tokens, and free drinks.

But here's what matters: is there anything about this new way of playing that can improve one's performance at the tables, or is it just a more efficient way to lose?

When I told a friend of mine about the 80% success rate I had encountered while playing the *targeted 6-8,* he speculated that the programming for the random number generator used for the game of craps might be flawed. See, in a normal gaming situation, every shooter has his own style. Some of them 'fix' the dice, others toss them lightly, while others hurl them with all their might. All these variations may take the game to a whole new level of randomness, and might not be accounted for with software that is programmed to produce only a general degree of randomness.

If there is even the slightest scrap of truth to that theory, there may be some serious implications to this. Any perceived weakness in a competitor is usually destined to be exploited mercilessly until the rules are changed.

You never know. There may be some changes ahead.

According to a piece in the July, 2000 issue of *Casino Player* magazine, the annual revenue for the online gambling industry by the year 2010 is estimated to be $90 billion. That figure presumes that it won't be regulated out of existence, or brought to its knees by computer viruses, or shut down by a gigantic asteroid that wipes out every living being on the face of the earth.

So, if you're opposed to online wagering, it may comfort you to know that you just might have that asteroid thing going for you, if nothing else.

Mind you, there is no real assurance that Internet gambling will still exist by the year 2010. Anything that explodes onto the scene so quickly runs the risk of embryonic burnout. Especially, in a world that doesn't yet trust the Internet, filled with bureaucracies that crave to tax and regulate it to death.

But even in the face of a recent bill submitted to Congress, which is intended to prohibit the use of credit cards or any other financial transaction for the purposes of gambling on the Internet, my money is on the survival of online gambling. I think it's here to stay, because it should be too firmly entrenched in the national soil by the time they figure out how to stop it.

Personally, I love online gaming. I love its accessibility and its efficiency. But I look at casinos and the games they offer in a much different light than most people.

As I've said, it is what you make it to be.

That is, until the asteroid hits.

PART III

PUTTING IT ALL TOGETHER

15

GETTING STARTED

Go slow, and expect setbacks.
—Paul Reiser, from
Mad About You

In most endeavors, *getting started* is the biggest hurdle to overcome. This is particularly true in matters that pertain to the exploitation of games of chance.

One such hurdle is that you haven't yet built up a monetary reserve, and this is not something money alone can solve. Even if you can get the money, it wasn't *won money*. It's more precious to you, for you know how hard you worked to get it. And, you haven't the confidence that comes from knowing that you got it by beating the casinos.

Because of this, you have to do things differently on the front end than after you've found your stride. You aren't immune to losses caused by flukes. They're going to hurt you, and could cause you to change your game plan.

The best way to prepare yourself for your debut on the casino stage is to practice with a friend, over and over again, all the bets and moves you expect to be making when you put your hard-earned money on the line for real.

If you're serious about making money in casinos, the first thing to do is get some scorecards printed up, so you can start collecting a database of table results. These can be used to make projections of how a strategy works in a live wagering situation. Never throw these table results away!

Next, I would recommend that you purchase a craps layout at a gaming supplies store for practice games of your own. Or, if you plan to play online, you can use their practice modes to accumulate some table results, and also to familiarize yourself with the numerical patterns. Continue on that basis until you've mastered the moves.

When your artificial gaming table produces patterns that cause losses, quit—just as you would in real life. Move away from the table and spend a few minutes doing something else. This is more important than people realize. To be truly prepared, you need to go through the same motions as in real life. If that is too much effort, then it might be time to acknowledge that this activity is not for you.

When you start making live bets, your focus should be on what you can learn from the experience rather than how much money you can make. Keep your sessions short, so you'll have time to analyze the results, rate the performance of your strategy, and evaluate *your own* performance.

Accept the fact that mistakes will be made. Try to uncover the reasons they occurred, and how you might avoid them in the future. After you've mastered them, however, don't be surprised if new ones move to the front.

Acclimating yourself to this life is done by keeping your sessions brief, and then assessing that experience. Little by little you'll come to understand the ways of the beast. At some point, you will feel ready to take him on. Your bets will then be larger, and you'll be playing more aggressively.

What you have to do will take time. As George Harrison said in his song, *Set on You:*

It's gonna take time;
a whole lot of patience and time.

WHAT IT TAKES TO WIN

*Develop a PHD attitude: Poor, Hungry and Driven; the
kind of attitude that will drive you to learn more and be better.*

—Rick Pitino
Success Is a Choice

There was a scene in the movie *Diamonds Are Forever*
where James Bond picks up the dice at a craps table and rolls a
10 as his point. He tells the dealer *"I'll take full odds on the 10,
$300 on the hardway, $250 on the eleven and the limit on all the
numbers; thank you very much."* Moments later, he walks away
with $50,000 profit and a hot babe on his arm who was obviously
attracted to his sudden wealth.

It's nice to dream, but we all know that the above is not an
accurate representation of a successful gambler. Not even close.
Even James knows better than to use such a reckless technique
unless he's playing with *someone else's money,* as was the case
in that movie.

Well then, what sort of picture accurately depicts the way a
successful gambler wins, and continues to win? And what did it
take for him to get there in the first place?

It all comes down to a simple concept: go for small gains,
until your winnings enable you to go for larger gains.

That's it. That's all you need to know to get started, to win,
and to succeed indefinitely. If you can maintain strict adherence
to that philosophy, you're there.

With every bet you make, you must stay focused on your end goal of being able to continue the effort. Meaning, protecting your bankroll is your utmost priority. What complicates the task, however, is the hardship of dealing with losses. It's always nice to win, but the losses send a powerful message: at that moment in time, you're a loser. It hurts. You're upset. You want to retaliate. You want to prove to the world that this is a fluke. You can win; you just need more time. More bets.

The people who run the casinos know of this effect on the people who play their games. They know that the wins are taken in stride, but they don't provide the commensurate lift to balance out the pain that the losses inflict upon the player. Consequently, the player tends to become obsessed with the idea that he has to compensate his losses immediately.

This is why the casinos win.

A disciplined player takes his losses in stride. He ignores the pain he endures. He keeps playing his game, same as before. He always comes back with a *measured* response.

This is much harder than it sounds, because your brain is sending you signals that you need to get back at the table that did that to you. And it's urgent.

To succeed, you have to rise above that mentality. You are the one in control. Not the table; not the casino. You will emerge victorious in the end, but it will be on your terms. Until you learn to see it that way, you'll be a fat target.

There was a time when I thought that gambling was simply a methodical process of turning over money. All I'd be doing is processing bets, as if in a factory. But I didn't foresee the way you feel when you've been dealt a tough loss that you thought you would win. It makes you angry. It makes you cringe inside. You feel sick. This was not supposed to happen. What are you going to do now?

Best thing to do when you feel that way is to leave the table and take a break. Cool off. Don't take it personally. The shooter didn't do that to you on purpose.

Take it in stride. Move on.

BUILDING A BANKROLL I
THE STAGES

We strain hardest for things which are almost but not quite within our reach.

—Frederick W. Faber

Your first task in the process of achieving a level of success as a player of casino table games is to build a bankroll. This is a project that has to take place in stages.

How many stages? As many as it takes to get you to where you're content with the monetary gains you seek. But be careful: it's not a matter up moving up slowly through the ranks. You're going to have frequent setbacks. When that happens, your best move is to abandon your lofty aspirations and retreat to a lower level, so as not to jeopardize your bankroll.

I recommend starting at the $5 level. This is the minimum level you'll find in most casinos, or online, for the game of craps. Give yourself two or three hundred dollars to start out with, and see if, over a period of time, you can double it. But even if you manage to succeed at this, don't think you can relax. The hardest part about this preoccupation is that, in fact, you can *never* relax. The moment you do, all hell will break loose.

If you should lose the two or three hundred dollars that you started with, you'll then be at a crossroads. What should you do? Start all over again, or abandon the pursuit? That's a question that only you can answer.

What you must *not* do in that situation, is think that your luck is bound to change, and push your bets to a higher level. This is a trap. Don't go for it.

I know it's hard to write off your losses and start out fresh, as if nothing had happened. You're upset about losing, and you want to get your money back as fast as you can. But you've got to remind yourself that this is why most gamblers lose in the end. They are victimized by their lack of self-restraint.

Most of today's gaming authors will tell you that craps is a *negative expectation game*. What they're saying, is that even if you have the will to overcome your compulsive tendencies, the house edge will get you in the end. I disagree with this, because I feel that one can become adept at spotting gaming trends, and if he confines his wagering activity to those times when the table is sending certain signals, he will win more than the normal share that is alloted to everyday gamblers. But never think for even an instant that it will ever be easy. You're going to be put to a new test every day, and if you aren't able to summon the appropriate quantity of discipline in each new case, you're going to end up as just another part of a frightening statistic.

Remember, the casinos are masters of illusion. They can make you think you're winning while they siphon money right out of your pocket, all day long.

One of your strongest lines of defense is your loss limits. Before starting out each day, you must put some serious thought into how much you will allow yourself to lose in the event things don't go as planned. Not only must you assign yourself a session loss limit, but also a daily loss limit. Then stick to it. If you don't do this every day, you're dead meat on a stick.

As you gain experience, you'll learn to stop *before* reaching your loss limit, because things aren't going well and you have the good sense to quit.

Those who succeed at casino table games possess a rare blend of qualities that enable them to take everything in stride. They don't get excited when they win, or upset when they lose. It's all part of the game.

BUILDING A BANKROLL II
THE FIVE RULES

Success seems to be largely a matter of hanging on after the others have let go.
—William Feather

Previously, it was established that in your effort to acquire a level of proficiency at the tables, you should dole out money to yourself in two or three hundred dollar increments. If you find that you're exhausting these amounts on a regular basis, you're going to have to take a hard look at whether or not you are suited for this type of endeavor.

I don't think you need to be investing time and money in something that proves to be a continual drain on your resources. But if you're doing okay, here are some operating guidelines that should be beneficial:

RULE 1: *When the tables give you a hard time, settle for whatever you can get.* Don't fight too hard, because you are not yet a match for such an accomplished adversary. Think of yourself as a thief, stealing valuables from the dragon's lair. Be thankful you got out of there alive.

RULE 2: *Your goals are modest. You're not seeking a big score.* Starting out, all you're going to do is test the water with a few $5 bets to see if you can get a nibble. If every chip you toss out sinks straight to the bottom, this is not a good sign. Move on to another table.

What you're attempting to do is like jumping onto a speeding train. At first, all you seek is to hang on and keep up with the flow of things. When you start getting regular returns, you'll know you're keeping pace with the table, for the moment. From there, try to get a feel for its destination.

RULE 3: *When a well-defined trend presents itself, move in slowly for the kill.* This is why you came: to catch the table whose trend is so pitifully obvious. A craps table where some lucky shooter rolls forty-five numbers, or one where ten consecutive shooters seven-out. Either one can be a gold mine to a seasoned player. When you find such a rare gem, start out conservatively, then use your winnings to methodically finance wagering increases.

RULE 4: *When that inevitable losing jag arrives, don't let yourself be swayed by other temptations.* If you're not doing well at craps, take a time out and do something else for a while. Then try again later. If it doesn't help, you may have to face the fact that this isn't your day to win. We all have days like that. But most important, don't use your losses as an excuse to head for the blackjack tables, for example, because you were desperate to find a game *where you could win.*

RULE 5: *Remember, if you maintain your discipline, you cannot fail in the long run.* This is what it comes down to: Can you maintain your discipline? If you can, you will succeed. If you don't, you'll fail. That's it.

What this means, in specific terms, is that you must never lose your cool. Never respond to the anger you may feel. And never think you're unbeatable. Hold back when losing, and press your advantage when winning.

There they are. The five rules. This isn't everything you need to know to succeed, but if you can remember these five, you'll be way ahead of the pack.

HOW MUCH CAN YOU MAKE?

It's not enough. It's never enough. The whole point of life is about wanting more.

—the Author

There is a prevailing notion that if you can make $5 a day in a casino, you can make $5000 a day. All it takes is bigger bets. That may, in fact, be why you purchased this book.

Although this book shows how to play casino table games, it's not a *get-rich* book. Even if you can succeed at the lower bet levels, all kinds of complications come into play when you try to maximize your success by betting larger.

For starters, you have to first obtain absolute proof that you can continue to win as you did before. Just because you showed a nice profit from your last fifty sessions, don't think that the next fifty will be as easy. Games of chance have a way of dishing out their biggest surprises when least expected.

Then there's the matter of overcoming problems associated with your comfort zone, as noted back in Chapter 6. It takes a lot of time and seasoning to adjust to higher betting levels.

Another thing to consider is bankroll. To support the effort to make $5000 a day, I would imagine that you'd need a bankroll in the neighborhood of $100,000. That's a conservative estimate. Chances are, you'd need more than that.

One of the biggest problems you'll face, however, is that your play will come under intense scrutiny. The casino personnel will be watching your every move like a hawk.

As noted in Chapter 4, your wins are causing someone else to lose, and nobody likes to lose. It matters not if you're playing a 'negative expectation game.' If you're taking their money on a regular and consistent basis, it's just a matter of time before they intervene. Sure, they expect a few players to win occasionally, but they're not in business to give money away.

In addition to the above, there's one more impediment to making the big bucks that is seldom, if ever, mentioned in books. This pertains to the psychology of gaming. If your main focus is on making money in casinos, the most cherished moment in your day will be when you stop playing, because finally, you don't have to put any more of your precious money at risk. Even the most accomplished gambler never feels truly comfortable as long as he has to keep putting his money on the line. He has enough respect for his adversary to stop challenging him *once he's gotten what he needs.*

Back in Chapter 13, I described a day in the life of one who plays table games professionally. On that day, I stopped playing after about two hours. Why did I stop when I was doing so well? Why didn't I go for more?

I stopped because I felt that to continue would be suicide. I'd had a good run. I knew the odds were due to turn against me. If I had decided to press on, I might have lost some key bets, and then feel a need to keep playing until winning back those losses. I might have ended up losing all that I'd won.

But what's the difference between playing for two hours a day on two consecutive days, and playing two sessions the same day? Isn't it the same? Not really. See, when you stop, you know that whatever you won will *stay won,* at least for the day. Finally, the tension, the dread of losing, the frustration of dealing with losses, and the anxiety you feel, slip away. Until the next time, you're at peace with the world. You've locked up your profit, and you know that your money is secure.

So, even though you may have the skill to make big money, you learn to be content with less.

As the saying goes, *less is more.* So true.

THE BUSINESS PLAN
THE SEVEN STAGES

Do it! Move it! Make it happen! No one ever sat their way to success.

—H. Jackson Browne, Sr.

Now that your possible expectations about casino gambling have been doused with the cold splash of reality, let us get back to the task at hand: putting the pieces together.

There is no strategy that's perfect for everyone. Some people prefer a generous win rate, because it is psychologically nurturing. But they must settle for low returns. Others may want to specialize in bets with higher payoffs.

In any case, you should take some time to think about what you really want to do. This calls for a *business plan.* The one I recommend has seven stages, noted below:

1) *The Selection Stage:* choosing a strategy that you like.
2) *The Collection Stage:* building a databank of table data.
3) *The Computation Stage:* performing trials on paper.
4) *The Rehearsal Stage:* practice sessions with a friend.
5) *The Live Trial Stage:* limited live betting at low levels.
6) *The Evaluation Stage:* analyzing that performance.
7) *The Live Betting Stage:* live gaming sessions.

FIGURE   30
The Seven Stages of the
Business Plan

THE SEVEN STAGES:

1) *The Selection Stage:* Before selecting a procedure to play, you must first ask yourself what kind of bet return appeals to you. Do you think you'd prefer playing favorites, where you win often but at a low price? Perhaps you'd rather be a longshot specialist, so you can get at those fat returns. Try to choose something at which you think you can excel.

Once you've settled on the type of bet return you would like, your next step is to pick a specific procedure. Figure 31, below, shows some procedural options:

Basic Line Betting	*Odds Betting*
Advanced Line Betting	*The Two-Number Don't*
Closed Progressions	*The Sister System*
MultiLine	*The Double Even*
The Random 22	*The Random Buy*
The Random Lay	*The Random Red*
The Random Five Eight	*The Random Six Nine*
Mixed Media	*The Selective Shooter*
The Targeted 6-8	*The Random Sister*

FIGURE 31
Gaming Options For Craps

Then there are strategies from other books, which you may find to be valid when squeezed through the *business plan* strainer. One that comes to mind is John Patrick's *Ricochet,* as shown in his book, *Advanced Craps.* Incidentally, I think his books are a good source for alternative procedures.

2) *The Collection Stage:* I've always felt that any information you can accumulate about probability expectation is vital, toward the end of helping you see what you're getting into. If you have an idea what win rate to expect, you'll be better prepared to deal with any complications that may arise.

Currently, there are system-tester books on the market, which show thousands of table results for craps. Or, you could make use of the practice modes at one of the online casinos, writing down all the table decisions as they accrue. After printing up the scorecards, fill them with this data.

3) *The Computation Stage:* At this stage, your mission is to find a strategy that works *on paper.* In doing this, avoid drawing premature conclusions. You might think that you've struck gold with something that works at the first fifteen tables, and then get very different results from the next fifteen.

But never confuse money made on paper with the real thing. While these trials help you see what to expect, things are different when real money is on the line.

4) *The Rehearsal Stage:* When you feel that you've latched onto something solid, it would be helpful to rehearse your act with a friend or partner. Done properly, this will simulate live gaming conditions, where you're making wagering choices against table decisions that are unknown in advance.

5) *The Live Trial Stage:* This is where you get down in the trenches and do it, in a tentative sort of way. In this mode, keep in mind that your goal is accumulating information more than money. Specifically, you need to know how well your strategy works, and how you perform in a live gaming situation.

6) *The Evaluation Stage:* Now, you need to take a step back and catch an overview of what you did and how you did it. Is your strategy holding up? If not, is the problem correctable? Are *you* holding up? Did you follow all the rules?

7) *The Live Betting Stage:* This is where it all leads. Your homework is done, and you're ready to go out and kick some butt. Just remember, *anything can happen in the short run,* so don't let the tables deceive you into thinking that whatever you're doing is terrible, or terrific. Give it time.

BANKROLL SAFEGUARDS

Man does not live long enough to profit from his faults.

—La Bruyère

In an episode of the TV sitcom *Suddenly Susan,* Susan's boss gambled away his Porsche, betting that his friend couldn't toss a poker chip into a beer glass, in one try. Later, he gambled away the company he owned.

In the movie *Lost in America,* Julie Hagerty gambled away $800,000 in a single night at a roulette table in Las Vegas while her husband slept. That money was meant to support the two of them for the rest of their lives.

In *Honeymoon in Las Vegas,* Nicolas Cage was about to call it quits in a poker game, when James Caan suckered him into raising the stakes, which resulted in Mr. Cage owing $50,000, an amount he could not repay.

This is why gamblers toss and turn at night. They know that in just a few minutes, they could lose everything that took them a whole lifetime to build. Scary? You bet.

What can you do to protect yourself from this possibility? Must you live your whole life in fear?

Enter *bankroll safeguards:* initiatives that hinder your own ability to get to your money. Measures *you* incorporate to keep you from draining all your bank accounts, should you suffer a *bodacious* lapse in discipline.

Can't happen to you? As I said before, and I'll say it again: you have the capacity to do this.

In considering the types of safeguards you'll need, you must project yourself into a crisis where you're forced to raise as much money as possible, as quickly as possible. Someone dear to you has just been kidnapped, and you need to get your hands on a lot of cash as fast as you can. Exactly how much could you raise in twenty-four hours, and how would you do it?

Include anything that could be liquidated in that period. Stocks, bonds, CDs, bank accounts, petty cash, and all the credit you could possibly get. Put all these figures on paper and then add them up. What's the total? Whatever it is, *that's how much you might lose in one day* if you don't take the time to assemble your own set of bankroll safeguards.

Some years ago I renounced the use of credit, except for a few revolving charge cards that are very seldom used. All my primary transactions are in cash, because that keeps me in touch with how much I'm spending, minute by minute. And when the wad of bills gets too big, I take the time to convert them to larger bills, or into high-value gaming chips. At all major casinos you can get tokens that are worth $5000 or more, which are very portable and instantly redeemable at the issuing casino twenty-four hours a day.

It shouldn't be hard to incorporate your own safeguards, but it should be taken care of before doing any serious gambling. For starters, avoid high-stakes poker games, because verbal bets are assumed to be binding. This is where people can lose things like cars and even houses—in a single bet.

Also, you may wish to consider making changes in how you pay for things. If you're currently using a lot of credit, it might be a good idea to start weaning yourself away from that. Of course, you should keep some credit cards for reservations or renting a car when traveling. But give yourself only as much spending power as what you think you can stand to lose in a day. And if your bank won't work with you to adjust your withdrawal allowances, consider switching banks.

Your end goal is to be where you can't raise more money in one day *than you can comfortably afford to lose.*

SUMMARY OF
GETTING STARTED

I have always felt that the most direct path to making money is by learning how to process and leverage money itself. There are a number of ways to do this, which include investing in the stock market, day trading, exploiting international currency fluctuations, purchasing municipal bonds, and working in the field of finance. But unless you have thousands of dollars to invest, you can never aspire to secure a foothold in any of these areas.

Casino gambling, when looked at as a means of turning over money, enables one to get started with a smaller investment. But the guiding principle for leveraging income is a constant for all of the above: seek small gains until you accumulate enough capital to go for larger gains. This was noted at the beginning of this chapter, but it is important enough to bear repeating.

It sounds easy enough, but putting it into practice is another thing altogether, because it's not a matter of progressing slowly in an upward direction. There will be setbacks that will compel you to swallow your losses, and consequently, lower your sights. Some people won't know how to deal effectively with these reversals of fortune. But it's an unavoidable part of the picture. You must adapt to this hardship, or abandon the quest.

If you seek to make a consistent income playing casino table games, you should know going in that the odds are strongly against you, and, that it will take a great deal of courage, perseverance, and determination.

Fact of the matter is: winning is not easy. Losing is not easy. If you're looking for *easy*, you won't find it here.

16

MISCELLANY

For the benefit of those who are unfamiliar with things like casino etiquette, tipping, and comps, this chapter has been added to shed some light on those and other subjects.

CASINO COMPS

Back in the days when Las Vegas casinos booked their own horseplaying bets, I witnessed something at the Barbary Coast casino that made an impression. A man had just won a $1000 bet on a 9–2 horse, which returned over $5500. I knew the guy was a regular, but wondered if casino management would ask him to take a hike after paying off the bet. Oh, how wrong could I be! Management broke out champagne and catered treats, treating him like he was king of the world. This was not at all what I expected to see. But looking back, I have to say that it made perfect sense. If they could get him to stick around, they would have a chance to win their money back. Lord knows, he can't keep winning forever!

The freebies he received are known as Complimentaries, but everyone calls them *comps*. They are part of a methodical reward system implemented by casino management to induce the players to keep gambling. The operative assumption is that the longer you play, the more you'll lose. But that's not how they sell the concept. To hear it from them, they're doing it because you're special, and deserve to be treated as such.

If you're in the habit of buying in at a table for $200 or more, it's only a matter of time before a floorperson will approach you and ask if you have a *player's card* (or whatever they call them), so that your betting action can be *rated*. If you act responsive, he or she will then try to sell you on the benefits of having this card.

What benefits? Well, you give the card to the floorperson as you make your buy-ins, and they keep track of your play. The longer you play at their tables, the more points you accumulate. In time, you can rack up enough points to pay for meals, hotel lodging, and items from their gift shop.

If you're a high roller, you could really cash in on all the enticements they're willing to offer, and you don't necessarily have to lose at the tables to qualify. We're talking luxury hotel suites, dining at its best, even free passage on cruise ships. All those things that epitomize the good life.

What's the catch? In this context, *free* is just another word for *stuff that's paid for five times over at the tables*. Meaning, you're expected to lose at least five times the value of the comps. But that's just part of the problem. When you give in to all that deleterious crap, you forfeit your *low profile* and your *anonymity*. And that might be all it takes to sabotage your efforts. The last thing you need is for them to get a handle on how much money you take out of their casino each day.

And there's more. In trying to earn complimentary points, you're likely to spend more time at the tables. You lose your focus. That's not good.

Nothing in this world is free. If you go after the comps, the greater chance is, you're gonna pay.

TIPPING

The free market works in accordance with the golden rule. The more we help others, the more we advance ourselves.

—Percy L. Greaves, Jr.

Everybody seems to have a different view on tipping dealers, so I'll just tell you what I do, and why.

Knowing that—at this writing—the rate of pay for dealers is about $7.00 an hour, I like to help out. They have a pretty tough job, and it seems to me that most players seldom tip. So, part of my motivation to tip derives from empathy.

My main reason for tipping, though, is purely selfish. If the dealers know I am prone to tip well, (I assume) they will be more courteous and accurate. They will be rooting for me to win, because when I do, there is an enhanced likelihood that I'll send a meaningful tip their way.

But I don't always tip. There are times when a table treats me so bad, it's just not in my heart. And I don't think the dealers expect one at times like that.

How much to tip, and when? At a craps table, I often tip as I go, and depending on how I did, perhaps again as I leave the table. The "as I go" tipping is always in the form of bets that I make for the dealers. For instance, during the come-out, I may toss some chips to the stickman and request, *"two-way craps."* This is universally understood to mean a bet for the player and another bet for the dealers as a toke. This bet, however, should not be confused with *three-way craps,* which covers the craps numbers 2, 3 and 12.

When I'm cleaning up because a shooter is making a lot of points, I frequently put down a *"line bet for the dealers,"* and may even hedge it with the *two-way craps* just described. If it seems like it's too late in the game for that, sometimes I place the point (or another number that's hitting) for the dealers. And let me tell you: I wish my own bets had as high a win rate as the ones I make for dealers. (But if I attempted to cash in on that, it would surely change my wagering impulses.)

At the end of a successful session, I usually give the dealers a little something. My standard tip ranges from $5 to $25, but I go outside that range when things go really well or really bad. That doesn't include the *as I go* tips, which are made primarily when I'm getting good service.

By the way, when you tip in the form of a wager, the dealers never leave it up beyond a single hit. If you toss a couple whites toward the stickman, saying *"two-way craps"* and it wins on that roll, the stickman assumes you'll want *your* bet repeated on the next roll, and he'll have the dealer give you $7. For the dealers' part of that bet, however, you'll hear something like *"Eight dollars and down for the dealers."* Even if your tip takes the form of a place bet (which is a continuous wager), there are only two things that can happen to that bet: 1) it will lose, or 2) it will win *once*. After the win, the bet and its profit go straight to the dealers' tip fund. There is *no chance* that a dealer's place bet will stay up to win as the bet was designed to be played. They want to get their money while they can, and leave the gambling to the customers.

As for the cocktail waitresses, I usually tip them a buck or two for each drink they bring, using whatever chips are handy. And this, again, is done for selfish reasons. When they're attuned to my drink preferences, some of them will bring me that drink without asking.

Whether to tip and the size is your call, but I recommend it. When you're up against such a powerful opponent, it sure is nice to feel that some of the enemy's warriors are actually rooting for your success.

CASINO ETIQUETTE

If you have no money, be polite.
—Danish proverb

What can I say about etiquette? I never give it a thought, unless I see some obnoxious clown making a scene. Only then do I think about it—just long enough to wonder why the concept of manners escapes him so exhaustively.

Escapes *him?* Did I say *him?* Come to think of it, I have to dig really deep into my memory banks to conjure an image of an obnoxious *her.* Seems like this sort of behavior is gender-biased, though I take no pleasure in admitting it.

Casinos try to project an image as a fun and exciting place, but sometimes a player who had too much to drink takes the party atmosphere too seriously.

For most of those who go to casinos, etiquette is a matter of common courtesy. For them, it's okay to get a little wild as long as they are somewhat sensitive to the reactions of others around them. But for a successful gambler, the rules are not the same. The casino may in fact be his place of employment, and drinking on the job is forbidden in any legitimate line of work. Serious gambling is no exception.

At all casino table games, the rules of etiquette are pretty simple. Treat the dealers and the players with respect and avoid behavior that is belligerent, pushy, or rude. If you get into some kind of dispute, be gracious. Be the peacemaker. Be the one to back down. Whatever the problem may be, nothing is worth the risk or indignity of being cast as the bad guy—by anyone who might be watching.

At craps, the rules are more complicated than for the other games. If you're not sure of something, take your cue from the other players. But here are some rules you should know, because they are enforced by casino personnel:

1) When holding the dice, keep your hand over the layout and do not switch them to the other hand. This helps assure the table crew that you're not a *dice mechanic* (one who replaces the official casino dice with a crooked pair).

2) Do not spend a lot of time fixing the dice or engaging in an elaborate ritual before throwing. The players and casino crew will be expecting you to roll the dice within two or three seconds after receiving them.

The following is a continuation of the list, but these are not really enforceable:

3) Try to get the attention of the dealer before tossing out chips for bets made through him.

4) Proposition bets should be made through the stickman, not the dealer, so try to make sure you have his attention before tossing your chips his way.

5) Unless you're shooting, do not hang your hands over the layout where they might end up in the path of the tumbling dice. And if you're the shooter and someone's hands are in the way, don't be afraid to call out, *"Hands up"* before throwing.

6) Don't force your way into a crowded table. If there isn't room for you to put your chips in a separate section of the chip tray, you probably don't belong there.

7) To keep the game moving, know the correct amounts for bets, odds, and payoffs.

8) Don't try to take the dice from the table. If you retrieve dice that flew off the table, return them promptly.

9) Try to be discreet about your wins and losses.

10) One last admonition: while on duty, the pros don't party, and they don't drink.

SECURITY

In Lyle Stuart's *Winning at Casino Gambling,* he talks about the dangers of exiting casinos in Atlantic City at night, inferring that there's a chance that someone's gonna shove a gun in your face. If I didn't know better, his words would make me paranoid as hell. Fortunately, I *do* know better.

This has never happened to me, in Atlantic City, Las Vegas or anywhere. I've spent hours just sitting on a boardwalk bench in Atlantic City after dark, and I've upped and downed the Las Vegas strip many times after midnight. Ain't nothing going on. I'd know it if there was.

I haven't studied the statistics, but I think that casino towns, especially near casinos, are some of the safest places in the U.S. They have their own police force (in uniform *and* plainclothes), and their cameras are everywhere. And although I used to feel a bit unsafe in certain casino parking garages, I have never been threatened, or encountered a dangerous situation. And I resent the implication that these places are unsafe. But then, I'm not in the habit of wearing tuxedos.

One must always be wary in today's world, especially when he carries a fair amount of cash. The hot tip is to dress down. There's a lot to be said for low profiles. If you project a modest image, you're much less likely to be a target. Just who're you trying to impress, anyway?

The guy with the gun?

If you're discreet about your winnings, dress down and don't drive a Jaguar, the guns have a remarkable tendency to disappear from the landscape.

To me, that's worth quite a bit.

RIGGED GAMES

I must complain that the cards are ill-shuffled, 'till I have a good hand.

—Swift

In the movie *Casablanca,* Rick, a nightclub owner, took pity on a young man, and told him to put all his roulette chips on one number. After that bet won (of course), Rick advised him to let all his winnings ride, and whaddya know—it won again!

That's the way casinos operate in the movies. But this is not to be confused with real life.

In the real world, a secret like that could never be kept from the media bloodhounds. After all, roulette dealers are real people like you and me, and all major casinos employ dozens of them. If the games were rigged, one of those dealers would squeal sooner or later. That would be the scoop of the century!

And then the casino would lose its dearest possession: its gaming license.

There is simply no good reason for any casino to take that kind of risk in a world with regulations that are a lot more strict than those in Morocco during the Nazi occupation.

Don't buy in to the idea that rigged games exist in casinos. They already have all the advantage they need.

Anything beyond that would be overkill.

EPILOGUE

I've always thought there's one thing that will really get you to heaven, and that is to have a compounded EPS growth rate of 15 percent.

—Financier Carl H. Lindner

One of the paradoxes of gaming is that although the casino is the opponent, to a pro, it is technically his employer. Against it he must win, but he needs it to stay solvent so he can *continue* to win. What it comes down to, is that he needs for it to *lose* against him, and *win* against the other guys.

How do you beat such a mighty adversary? You've got to study the table before making an investment, until you get a sense of what it will do next. The way you win at the tables is to tailor your play to results the table is naturally disposed to give. That's all you have to do.

But it's not easy. The fact is, it's hard. It's full of surprises. See, the casinos have created the perfect environment for your destruction. You've got to run through their gauntlet, oblivious to all their slings and arrows. You've got to rise above it all. You don't see a thing, hear a thing, feel a thing.

Just like a banker or financier, your job is to squeeze out a moderate profit as you turn over money. Your job is harder than that of a financial consultant, for you have to make split-second decisions, all day long. But all you are really trying to do is to *keep the flow of money under control.*

If you can do that, you're there.

Stay focused. Dance the dance. Gamble to win.

SCORECARD PLATES

Figures 32 through 34 were added to enable you to print up your own scorecards, which help organize the incoming data while at the tables. It is recommended that you have Figures 32 and 34 printed at full size and then bound into pads of 50 sheets apiece, as described in Chapter 12. Figure 33 was designed to be enlarged to 200% of its actual size, so that it ends up filling up a letter size (8½ x 11) sheet of paper. To enhance the clarity of the two areas used for inputing table data, you may wish to paste up copies of Figure 32 over those areas, and then use that finished result as the new original.

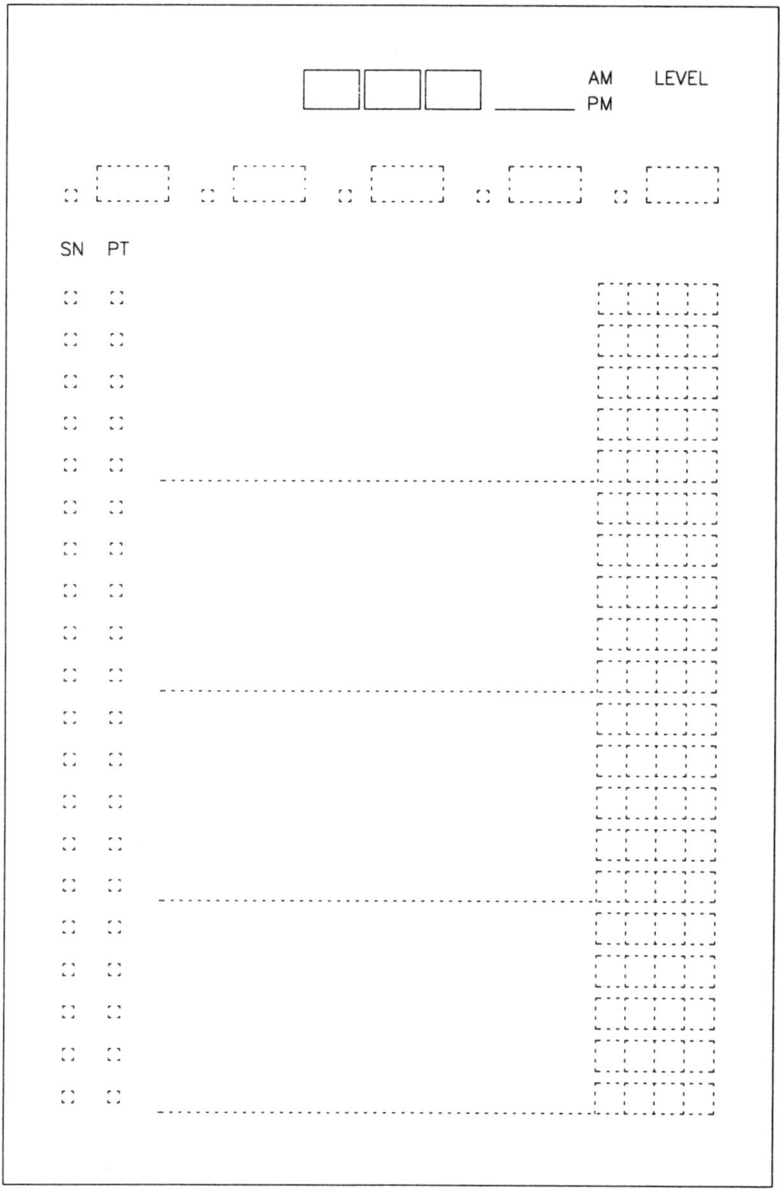

FIGURE 32
The Basic Scorecard

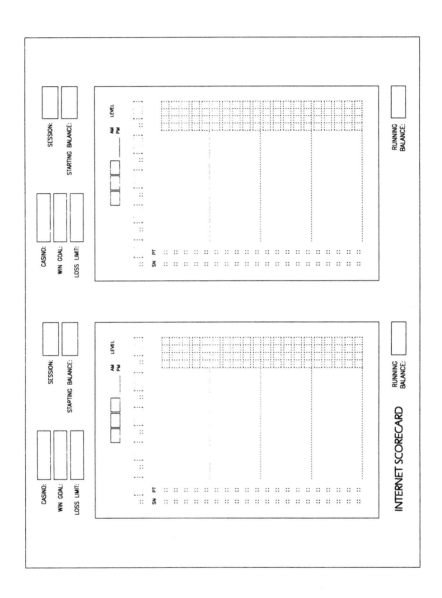

FIGURE 33
The Internet Scorecard
(Reduced Layout)

FIGURE 34
The Statistics Scorecard

GLOSSARY

CRAPS & GENERAL GAMING TERMS

Ace-Deuce   A term for the number 3 on a pair of dice.

Aces   A term for the number 2 on a pair of dice.

Action   Betting activity, as in a casino.

Advantage   See *House Edge.*

Analysis Stage   Referred to in this book as a period when one is evaluating table conditions in a casino.

Anti-Martingale   The opposite of the *Martingale* system in gaming. This one involves doubling the bet size after winning, as opposed to doubling after a loss.

Any   An abbreviated command for the bet *Any Craps.*

Any Craps   A one-roll proposition bet that pays 7–1 and covers the numbers 2, 3 and 12. Normally played as a hedge to protect the pass line bet during the come-out.

Any Seven   A one-roll proposition bet that pays 4–1 when a 7 is rolled. Also referred to as *Big Red.*

Any Seven Parlay   See *Big Red Parlay.*

Auxiliary Bet   Referred to in this book as a bet that falls outside the scope of the main wagering strategy, but is permitted to exploit a conspicuous table condition.

Back Line   A term for the *don't pass* betting area of a craps layout, or, referring to that type of betting activity.

Bank Craps   The game of *craps,* where players bet against the house instead of each other.

Bankroll   the amount of money one sets aside specifically for the purpose of placing bets at games of chance.

Bareback Betting without the accompaniment of a hedge bet as protection against losing to a longshot. Generally applies to situations involving large, odds-on wagers.

Bet An amount of money used for speculative investment at a game of chance. Also called *wager.*

Bet the Farm To risk a considerable sum of money, likely to overextend the player in the event of a loss.

Betting Strategy A technique employed by a bettor which aspires to outperform random wagering.

Bettor One who places wagers or bets.

Big Eight A continuous wager that pays even money if the number 8 is rolled before a 7.

Big One A gaming term for $1000.

Big Red See *Any Seven.*

Big Red Parlay See Chapter 10 (page 141).

Big Six A continuous wager that pays even money if the number 6 is rolled before a 7.

Bill A gaming term for a $100 bill.

Black A $100 gaming token, which is issued, and used as money, in a casino.

Blacks Casino gaming chips or tokens having a face value of $100 within the gaming area of the issuing casino, so called because of their color, black.

Boxcars A craps term for the number 12 on a pair of dice. Also called *Midnight.*

Boxman The seated member of the craps table crew who is responsible for supervising the game.

Box Number Any of the following numbers: 4, 5, 6, 8, 9 or 10 at a craps table. This grouping represents all point numbers, and all *place bet* numbers.

Buy-In The monetary figure exchanged for casino chips at the commencement of table game wagering.

Buy Bet An alternative to *place bets* at the craps table, often preferred by players betting on the 4 or 10, because the 5 percent commission is a better deal than the 6.67% vigorish of the place bets for those two numbers.

Cashier   One who handles monetary transactions in a casino, such as exchanging gaming tokens for cash, or processing payments for cash advances or markers.

Cashier Cage   The area where the *casino cashier* works, so called because of the bars or glass partition that customarily separate the cashier from the public.

Casino   1) A building, or area within a building, where games of chance are offered to the public. 2) A term indicating the *house,* the entity players bet against.

Casino Manager   The executive in charge of all operations within a casino.

Center Field   A term used to indicate the number 9 at the craps table, so called because its position is in the center of the string of numbers representing field bets.

Change Color   To convert casino gaming chips to larger or smaller denomination chips.

Chart   1) To analyze the results or numerical patterns that accrue at a casino table game. 2) To document those results on a sheet of paper, for immediate or later use.

Check   A casino gaming chip or token, which is used as money in a casino.

Chip   A gaming token, used as money in a casino.

Choppy   A casino table trend or pattern that is abnormally inconsistent or difficult to predict.

CL   An abbreviation for *Cumulative Loss.*

Closed Progression   A series of bets that increase in size as losses continue, until the fixed upward limit is reached.

Cluster Principle   A theory, advanced by the author of this book, which states that: *For every absence of a probable event, there is an equivalent compression of subsequent events.*

Cold Table   A table that favors the *don't pass* bettor.

Cold Dice   The term used to attribute a trend (favoring the back line bettor) to the dice rather than the table.

"Color"   A term used by some players to alert the dealer that they are leaving the table, and wish to have their gaming chips converted to higher denominations.

"Color In" See *Color.*

Come Bet A craps bet that is identical to a pass line bet, except for *when* the bet is made.

Come Box The marked area of a craps table where a *come bet* is placed.

Come-Out The time between when a craps shooter first acquires the dice, and rolls a point number.

Come-Out Bet A *pass line, don't pass, come* or *don't come* bet, during the *come-out* period.

Comfort Zone The range of bet levels at which the player feels comfortable with the monetary risk involved.

Commission A fee charged by casinos for selected bets.

Comp A *complimentary;* a signed ticket that entitles the player to free meals, lodging, or the like. Offered by casinos as a reward for playing time accrued at the tables.

Complimentary See *Comp.*

Compulsion Defined in this book as the inherent part of human nature to become reckless or irrational with one's money in certain gaming situations.

Continuum Defined in this book as the ongoing sequence of betting opportunities in casinos, giving players insufficient time to make intelligent betting decisions.

Contra D'Alembert The inverse of the *D'Alembert* system for even money wagers. See Chapter 8.

Controlled Greed Defined in this book as the paradoxical attitude that can enhance one's chances for success: *A passionate desire for a sensible bet acquisition.*

CP An abbreviation for *Cumulative Profit.*

Craps 1) A casino table game played with a pair of dice. 2) A dice roll of 2, 3 or 12 at the game of craps, which causes a loss to *pass line* bets when rolled during the come-out.

Crew Casino personnel who staff a craps table.

Customized Scorecard A card for charting table results, which has been designed specifically for that need.

Dagwood Edge A theoretical player advantage that reads: *Keep the game moving until the preferred side wins.*

D'Alembert System   A technique designed for even-money wagers that calls for bet fluctuations at predetermined intervals. Also called the *Pyramid.*

Dealer   The casino staff member who runs a table game or assists in its execution.

Deuce   The number 2, on a pair of dice.

Dice   A pair of six-sided cubes, marked on all sides with dots representing numbers, used at craps and other games.

Dice Combinations   The total of the 36 ways the numbers 2 through 12 can be rolled from a pair of dice.

Dice Fixing   Setting the dice in a fixed position prior to the roll, in the hopes of influencing the dice result.

Dice Mechanic   A player who attempts to cheat at a dice game by switching or manipulating the dice.

Die   The singular of *dice.*

Disk   See *Puck.*

Dollar   A casino term for a $1 or $100 gaming token.

Don't Bettor   A craps player who specializes in wagering against the point and/or other point numbers, through the use of *don't pass, don't come* or *lay* bets. Also called a *back line bettor,* or *wrong bettor.*

Don't Come Bet   The opposite of a *come* bet at the game of craps, in the same way that a *don't pass* wager is the opposite of a *pass line* wager.

Don't Come Box   The marked box on a craps layout in which a *don't come* bet is placed. Also, the place where the *puck* is stored before the point is established.

Don't Pass Bet   The opposite of a *pass line* wager at craps. This bet wins if the shooter rolls a 7 before rolling a repeat of the point number, but during the come-out, a 7 or 11 results in a loss; a *craps* 2 or 3 wins, and the 12 is a push.

Double Odds   *Free Odds,* of an amount that is double the size of the *pass line* bet at the game of craps.

Downside   A negative aspect or occurrence.

Dry Bet   An imaginary bet, which is made to postulate a hypothetical result at a game of chance.

Easy See *Easy Way.*

Easy Way At craps, a term that indicates that a dice result was a common roll of the number 4, 6, 8 or 10, as opposed to the *hardway,* which occurs only through 'doubles.'

Edge See *House Edge.*

Even Money A bet return that pays 1–1 (which doubles the size of the original wager).

Favorite A term used in horseplaying, sports betting and competitions in general, which indicates the probable winner in the opinion of the oddsmaker or the public in general.

Field Bet A single-roll bet at craps that returns even money if a 3, 4, 9, 10 or 11 is rolled, 2–1 if a 2 is rolled, and (depending on the casino) either 2–1 or 3–1 if a 12 is rolled.

Flat Bets A term used in this book that indicates a string of bets that do not fluctuate in size.

Floorperson A roving troubleshooter who supervises all the games in the pit to which he is assigned.

Free Odds A supplemental bet to a *pass line, don't pass, come* or *don't come* bet at craps, available only after the point has been established. Named *Free Odds* because the risk to the player is in exact proportion to the probability (odds) for that bet to win; therefore, it carries no *house edge.*

Front Line The *pass line* at a craps table. A *front line bettor* is one who plays the *pass line.*

Gambler One who puts money at risk for speculative gain, either as a recreational pastime or as a vocation.

Gambling The act of risking money at games of chance or any other speculative venture.

Gaming Associated with gambling.

Gaming Commission A state regulatory agency that is responsible for licensing casinos, monitoring casino cash flow, and fielding customer questions and comments.

Gaming Specialist A gambler who specializes in certain casino table games.

Greens Value chips that are used for table game play, which have a face value of $25. Also called *quarters.*

Hard   The term for a craps roll of the dice that was produced through 'doubles.' If the stickman announces *"Number 8, hard,"* that tells you that the dice read 4 and 4.

Hardway Bet   A continuous bet at craps that pays 9–1 if a *hard* 6 or 8 (bet independently) appears before a 7 or an *easy* roll of that number. For a *hard* 4 or 10, the payoff is 7–1.

Hedge   See *Hedge Bet.*

Hedge Bet   A supplemental wager, smaller than one's primary bet but paying higher odds, designed to protect the bettor against a loss attributed to a longshot.

Hedge Bettor   One who advocates and plays *hedge bets* in an attempt to mitigate the downside.

High   A craps request for an extra unit of coverage on one of the *horn* numbers. Example: *"Horn, high eleven."*

High Roller   One who frequently places large bets.

Hop   A craps one-roll bet on a dice combination, exactly as spoken. *"5 and 3 on the hop"* is a request for a bet on a dice result that reads 5 and 3. Hop bets are usually available only in Nevada, and generally pay 15–1.

Hop Hardway   A hop bet on a dice combination that can be rolled only one way, which generally pays 30–1.

Horn Bet   A one-roll proposition bet at craps that covers four numbers, 2, 3, 11 and 12, with four betting units. It returns roughly 15–1 for a 3 or 11, and 30–1 for a 2 or 12.

Horseplaying   Speculating (betting) on thoroughbred race horses, usually at a racetrack.

Hot Dice   A craps term for dice that are passing (succeeding in making the established points).

Hot Table   A craps term used to indicate a table where the dice pass consistently.

House   A casino; the entity players bet against.

House Advantage   See *House Edge.*

House Edge   The statistical advantage enjoyed by casinos, derived by paying off winning bets at a rate below the amount that would equitably compensate the risk involved. Also referred to as *Advantage, House Advantage, Vigorish* and *Vig.*

Imposed Velocity   The term used in this book to describe refuge from the perils of *Continuum:* to impose a pace of betting activity controlled by the player instead of the casino.

Junket   A chartered trip to a casino that is priced below the market value, because participants are expected or required to spend time gambling (and therefore, losing).

Lay Bet   1) A *free odds* bet made as a supplement to a *don't pass* bet. 2) An independent bet against a point number, for which a 5% commission is charged by the casino.

Lay Odds   To add *free odds* to a back line wager.

Layout   The printed felt or material that represents the area where bets are positioned at a casino table game.

Lay Wager   See *Lay Bet.*

Let It Ride   To add the proceeds of a winning bet to the previous one, forming a new, larger bet. Also called *parlay.*

Little Joe   A craps term for a dice roll of 4.

Longshot   A bet that (statistically) has a small chance to win, but offers the potential for a high return.

Longshot Specialist   One who specializes in playing bets that carry a high payoff relative to the bet size.

Loss Limit   A monetary boundary applied to a bankroll which is not to be exceeded. Designed to protect the player from making foolish or impulsive wagering choices.

Martingale   A system, usually applied to even money bets, which involves doubling one's bet size with each loss, as often as necessary in an attempt to recoup previous losses.

Midnight   A craps term for a dice roll of 12.

Mini-Martingale   A variation of the *Martingale* system, which calls for one to abandon the series and write off the loss if a win is not produced from one of its limited stages.

Mixed Media   The term used in this book to mean a group of procedures that form a larger strategy. See Chapter 10.

Multi-Line   A procedure for craps, advocated in this book, which involves *line* and *come* bets.

Multiple Parlay   A parlay that exceeds one stage.

Natural   A dice roll of a 7 or 11 during a come-out.

Negative Trend   Defined in this book as *the conspicuous absence of a gaming event.* See Chapter 3.

Nickel   A gaming token having a face value of $5, used for placing bets. Also called a *Red.*

Odds   1) The statistical probability for an event to occur, often applied to casino games. 2) A term sometimes used to mean the *House Edge.* 3) The command to let the dealer know that the chips tossed his way are to be applied toward *free odds* for a *come* or *don't come* bet.

Odds Betting   A craps procedure for *line bets* that involves playing the *pass line* and *don't pass* simultaneously during the come-out, to abate come-out losses. See Chapter 9.

Odds-on   A bet that returns less than even money, usually associated with racetrack wagering.

Off   1) The rendering inactive of a craps bet (so that it is not subject to a win or loss). 2) The command a player uses to instruct the dealer that he wants his bet or bets to be rendered inactive until further notice.

On   1) An active craps bet. 2) The command a player uses to instruct the dealer that he wants his bet or bets re-activated after being shut *Off.*

One-Roll Bet   At craps, a bet that will either win or lose on the next roll, such as a field bet or proposition bet.

One-Shot   Defined in this book as a solitary wager or brief betting series that attempts to hit a wagering target with pinpoint precision. Also called a *surgical strike.*

1-2-3-4 System   A closed progression comprised of four bets that increase in size after each loss, until the last stage is reached or a win occurs. See Chapter 8.

On The Hop   See *Hop.*

Oscar's Grind   One of the more effective systems for even money bets known to gamblers. See Chapter 8.

Parlay   1) A bet comprised of its original amount, plus its winnings, forming a new, larger bet. 2) To place such a bet.

Pass Line   The centerpiece bet at craps, in which players seek the repeat of the point number before a 7 is rolled.

Past-Posting The illegal act of placing or increasing a bet after the wagering result is known.

Patrick System A technique devised especially for the *don't bettor,* to help such a player abate losses during the come-out phase. Invented by author John Patrick.

Payoff The proceeds of a successful bet.

Percentage A term sometimes used to mean *House Edge.*

Pit An area of a casino surrounded by gaming tables.

Pit Boss The casino executive in charge of the pit.

Place A craps wager. See *Place Bet.*

Place Bet A craps wager on one of the six point numbers, which pays 6–5 for a 6 or 8, 7–5 for a 5 or 9 and 9–5 for a 4 or 10, if such number is rolled before a 7.

Place Number One of the six numbers (4, 5, 6, 8, 9 & 10) that represents a place bet at a craps table.

Player One who risks money at games of chance, such as those offered in a casino.

Player's Edge Defined in this book as the aspects of table game play that benefit the player that serve as a counterweight to the casino advantage known as the *House Edge.*

Point At craps, one of six numbers (4, 5, 6, 8, 9 or 10) that the shooter rolls on the come-out and must roll again before a 7 to win.

Positive Trend Defined in this book as the *presence* of a conspicuous trend or gaming event. See Chapter 3.

Press 1) To increase the size of a wager, often using the proceeds of a successful bet to do so. 2) A verbal request for the dealer to increase a bet amount.

Press It Up A verbal command to a dealer to increase the size of a bet.

Professional Gambler One whose primary source of income is derived from gambling.

Profit The amount that is won from a single wager, or, an amount won over a period of time.

Progression A series of bets that increase in size until a win occurs, at which time a new series may begin.

Proposition Bet Any one of several craps bets positioned in the center of the layout, promoted by the *stickman*.

Puck A disk used to mark the point at a craps table, which is white on the *On* side, and black on the *Off* side.

Push A tie, at a casino table game.

Quarter A *generic* gaming chip having a face value of $25, used for table game play. Also called a *Green*.

Racetrack In this book, the term is meant to apply only to thoroughbred racetracks.

Rail A channel or pair of channels carved into the armrest of a craps table, where players store their gaming chips.

Random A term used in this book to denote a solitary bet or brief wagering series.

Random Walk A demonstration of the *Law Of Averages* in matters of chance. See Chapter 3.

Reality Check A procedure for monitoring one's behavior in a casino, advocated in this book. See Chapter 7.

Recreational Gambler One who gambles for recreation or sport, relying primarily on luck.

Regression A bet that is smaller in amount than a previous successful wager.

Repeat Table Defined in this book as a craps table having a tendency to produce repetitious patterns. See Chapter 11.

Right Betting 1) Betting the *pass line* at craps. 2) Betting on any of the craps wagers that are vulnerable to the seven, such as *place bets, buy bets* and *field bets.*

Right Side The *pass line* and associated bets; one of the two sides that represent the primary bet opposites at the game of craps. Also referred to as the *Do Side* or the *Front Line.*

Roll 1) The act of throwing the dice at the game of craps. 2) A single throw of the dice at craps. 3) The total number of throws made by the player in possession of the dice.

Scared Money Money put at risk by a player that is part of a fund insufficient for the task.

Scorecard A card or piece of paper used to chart gaming results, as a means of identifying trends at that table.

Selective Shooter   A procedure that involves betting on one's own rolls (only) at a craps table. See Chapter 10.

Series   A progression or group of wagers that complete a betting cycle.

Session   1) The period of time a player spends placing bets at a casino table game. 2) The duration of a riverboat cruise, where live gaming is offered to the passengers.

Settle For 90   Noted in this book as sound betting advice: *Don't obsess over the need to win an arbitrary amount; take what comes and be thankful it wasn't a loss.*

Seven-out   To roll a 7 before repeating the point at a craps table, causing forfeiture of the dice. A *seven-out* causes a loss for *pass line* bettors and a win for *don't pass* bettors.

Shift Boss   The executive in charge of operations within the casino during his work shift.

Shill   One hired by a casino to play table games, as a means of attracting casino patrons to a game.

Shoot   1) To roll the dice at a craps table. 2) The sum of a craps shooter's rolls.

Shooter   The craps player in possession of the dice.

Singles   The term for $1 gaming chips.

Sister Numbers   Dice results that have the same statistical probability. Example: 6 is the sister of 8, because both can be rolled in exactly five different ways. See Chapter 5.

Sister System   A craps procedure, invented by the author, that involves sporadic wagering on the sister to the *point* number. See Chapter 9.

Soft   A synonym for a type of dice result referred to as *easy,* at the game of craps. See *Easy Way.*

Stake   Money risked on a wager, or, the bankroll used to finance that activity.

Statistical Casino Advantage   See *House Edge.*

Stickman   The craps dealer who hawks *proposition bets* and controls the flow of the dice with a long stick.

Streak   1) A string of consecutive gaming decisions of the same result. 2) A string of consecutive wins or losses.

Surgical Strike   A synonym for a *One-shot,* defined in this book as a single wager or limited wagering series, placed at random at a casino table game. See Chapter 10.

System   A structured wagering procedure that aspires to outperform random wagering.

Table Game   Any one of several casino games, including *craps, roulette, blackjack, baccarat,* and *poker.*

Table Limit   Another term for *Table Maximum.*

Table Maximum   The maximum figure allowed for bets at a casino table game, usually noted on a small sign near the dealer. Note: Sometimes the casino personnel raise this limit for brief periods, at a player's request.

Table Minimum   The minimum figure allowed for a bet at a table game. Not always applicable, however, to secondary bets, such as *proposition bets* at craps.

Table Temperature   The disposition of trends occurring at a table game, usually attributed to craps tables. A *cold table* is one that favors *back line* bettors. See Chapter 11.

Table Trend   A conspicuous pattern of results occurring at a casino table game.

Take Odds   To add *free odds* to a *front line* wager.

Three-Way Craps   A *hedge* bet that covers the three *craps* numbers 2, 3 and 12 with three chips, and pays relative to the odds for each of those numbers.

Toke   A tip to a dealer or casino employee.

Token   Another name for gaming chip, though commonly associated with the metal type used in slot machines.

"Too Tall"   An expression often heard from the *stickman* at a craps table, which indicates that one or both of the dice landed in a player's rail.

Trend   See *Table Trend.*

Trial   An example or attempt.

Trigger   A gaming result that serves as the signal to place a bet or commence a wagering progression.

Two-Way Craps   A craps term for a bet comprised of two parts, one for the player and one for the dealers. See Chapter 5.

Vig   An abbreviation for *Vigorish*.

Vigorish   See *House Edge*.

Wager   A bet; money put at risk at a game of chance.

Warm   A gaming term associated with a craps table or pair of dice, indicating a trend favoring *right* bettors.

Whale   An insider's term for a *high roller* who is inclined to risk huge sums of money playing casino games.

White   A gaming chip with a face value of $1. Also called a *single*. Note: some casinos use a color other than white for their $1 chips, in which case the term may not apply.

Win   1) To profit from a successful wager. 2) A successful wager, series, session, or day.

Win Goal   A predetermined monetary goal set by players, at which point no more money, or a sharply reduced amount, is put at risk.

Working   1) A craps term for wagers that are active. 2) A verbal command to a craps dealer to re-activate a player's bets that had been shut *Off.*

World Bet   A five-unit craps bet that combines the *Any Seven* bet with the four parts of a *Horn* bet, paying in accordance with the odds for each component.

Wrong Bettor   See *Don't Bettor*.

Yo   1) A craps term for a dice roll of 11. 2) A bet made on that number, frequently made during the come-out.